HITMAN FOR

Christ

Frank Dimercurio

A servant of the Lord

ISBN 978-1-0980-7636-8 (paperback)
ISBN 978-1-0980-8184-3 (hardcover)
ISBN 978-1-0980-7637-5 (digital)

Christian Faith Publishing, Inc.
832 Park Avenue
Meadville, PA 16335
www.christianfaithpublishing.com

Printed in the United States of America

Written with much love for Virginia (Jinny) Dimercurio, my wife.

Contents

꩜ ◎ ꩜

Rosalia and Alphonzo Dimercurio, my parents

1

Dedication

My father, Alphonse Mercurio, was forced to change his name later in his life because of an unscrupulous cousin who was on the FBI's radar. This cousin who shared the same name caused all kinds of problems for my dad, both legally and, more importantly, with my mom. Apparently, while he was at work one day, the FBI showed up at their house and asked if my Dad was home. They were arresting him for fraud and a boatload of other charges. They claimed he stole fur coats and diamonds and ran up credit cards to buy expensive gifts for his girlfriends. Since my father was not home, they left but said they would be back.

When my father came home that night, it had seemed to him, worse than facing an army of agents. My mother was ready to kill him. How could he pretend to be just a poor working stiff and buy stuff for his girlfriends. She knew better, but she could be of the mentality at times to shoot first and ask questions later. Faced with all these accusations, he knew at once who they were after. In the Italian culture, the name Mercurio is a lot like the name Smith in the USA. Michael is the American version of Mercurio. In fact, Mercurio was a first name in Italy. When the immigrants arrived at Ellis Island— mostly with little paperwork, if they had any at all—they spoke little English. When asked for their name, they would reply Mercurio or of Mercurio. Depending on who was working the reception desk that day, their name could be recorded as just about any version of the name Mercurio. Some were given the name twice such as Mercurio Mercurio. Some would be registered as Di Mercurio, Demercurio, or Dimercurio. It did not matter to them, they made it to America. That was more important. They wanted to work and make a better life for their families.

My father told my mom not to worry, that he was going to fix this. He knew a guy who knew a guy who could get things done. Every Italian knew a guy who knew a guy who could get things done. This guy fixed the problem. He had my father legally change his name to the name given to his family at Ellis Island. His name was now Alphonse Dimercurio. My father was the oldest in his family and had several brothers. Apparently, they also knew a guy that knew a guy who could fix things so they had their names changed also. The problem was that while they all had the same parents, none of them spelled their last names the same.

I was born before the "fix" was in so I had Mercurio on my birth certificate for my last name and went by this name all the way through high school. When my father died, I wanted his last name so I took it upon myself to have the name changed. I did not have a guy who knew a guy so I did it myself and just filled out the paperwork. Therefore, I come to you today as Frank Dimercurio. Well, Frank Michael Dimercurio is my full name. Could not forget the Michael. You think this was confusing, you should have tried to live this life.

You are where you are in life by the choices you make. If you don't like where you are. Make different choices.

Saturday mornings at home were not always fun for my mom and sisters as we were growing up. For me, it was the day I looked forward to the most. My dad did not have to work most Saturdays. We used to sit at the kitchen table for hours and talk and talk, just the two of us. My sisters and mom dreaded it. We would argue, yell, and fight in their words, but my dad and I, well, we understood each other. We were passionate in our own beliefs. Granted, it could get testy at times, but we loved it. I was in my mid-teens. Mind you, most kids could care less about talking to their parents. On Saturday mornings, I had the attention of the smartest man I would ever know. The man I would use as a model to form my life after. I set my life goal back then to someday become just half the man he was. He was known as Big Al to his friends, coworkers, and neighbors. To me, he was not just big. He was a giant of a man who possessed more strength, wisdom, and knowledge than any man I would ever know. He was the walking, talking embodiment of what I would later find out of God's holy word tells us to be, though, to my knowledge, he never even opened the Bible. He could barely read.

He was a very humble man and while he was proud of me, he would become furious that I could see him in such an adoring manner. I think he only finished as far as fifth grade in school. He had difficulty with reading and math but insisted that I take my education seriously. He even made me promise him that I would go to college and get a diploma, something no other person had done up to that point in my family. It really pissed him off when I would say something like, "Why do I have to go to school? Look how successful you have become, and you never went." He would erupt, he worked for Stroh Brewery in Detroit, Michigan, where he delivered cases of beer to local stores. He was a bookmaker on the side. Not the kind of book maker you would think of. A numbers guy, they called themselves.

In the post-World War II days, people of the Depression era would pick their favorite three numbers in a lottery and get paid $600 to one for every bet they made that "came in." Sellars of hope. At some point, it sickened my dad that some of these people would play the numbers instead of buying their kids shoes or even food. Choices, bad choices kept people in bondage and poverty. The government condemned this gaming. Laws were enacted to put the numbers takers and gamblers in prison for peddling this false hope. This added to the excitement of getting away with something. One day, some "genius" in the government decided to just legalize betting, promote it, make billions of dollars. Hell, they even hired a marketing firm to make it look sexier. Thus was the birth of the lottery. The repeal of prohibition was the precursor to this. Legalized casino gambling, recreational drugs, red light districts for prostitution would follow.

Being raised in the Italian culture, there was a natural mistrust for government. Nothing good ever came from the government, any government. They would take and take. If you ever needed justice, you would get left out in the cold. However, if any other country tried to mess with ours, there would be hell to pay. The Italian people were fiercely loyal to their American Dream. I once found myself extremely frustrated later in life when an apparent injustice had taken place to one of my family members. I received a very honest and worthwhile piece of advice from an assistant prosecutor I befriended. He said to me in the midst of my rage, "Frank, if it is justice you seek, stay out of the system."

I would never forget that advice. The point I am trying to make is you always have choices. This simple truth was first taught to me by my father at a young age and later in life by my wife Jinny.

> *You are where you are in life by the choices you make. If you don't like where you are, make different choices.*

2

Gangster Wannabe or Boy Goes to College

I never backed down from a fight in my life. I never started a fight in my life either. I had gotten rather good with my fists too. I know now the reason people resort to using their fists is that they lack the intellect to settle things with wisdom and words. I developed a distain for people who would take advantage of other creatures, especially children. They call it bullying now. I had one word for it then and now: *bullshit*. I was strong—tough, by most standards. I found myself fighting bullies all the time. I could give a rip about the consequences. If you were going to hurt someone I cared about, I would bust your head. I developed a reputation as someone not to be messed with. Little did I know, I became a hitman.

My father saw this tendency in me. "Develop your brain, not your brawn," he would preach to me after I would come home bloodied up…again. "If all you are about is muscle, this will break down some day, and you will have nothing left to rely on." I found out that his real fear was about the gangster mafia mentality I was developing. He suffered heart disease. As he got sicker, our "talks" became more and more frequent. He used to warn me, "As soon as I die, they are going to come after you. The mob bosses, that is. It is going to seem real flattering at first. They will throw money, cars, and women at you, but it is a trap. They want to control you. Eventually, they will get you to do something they can hold over your head for the rest of your life. They will bury you by making you do things for them, horrible things, while they keep their hands clean. When they are done with you, they will discard you like a used rag. You will not be able to live with yourself. Killing yourself will seem like your best option. If you ever want to sleep at night, do not go down that road."

On the day before he died of a massive heart attack in my arms, as the rest of my family sat by his bedside, he asked me to take him for another ride in the car. I took him to the places we enjoyed together, mostly at the water's edge. He got out of the car and sat on the edge of a boat down at Tommy's Marina. He told me to sit next to him.

"I have something I need to tell you. Promise me you will take care of your mother and sisters. Frank, you can have all the women you want in life, but you will only have one mother. Treat her like a queen." He hesitated as if trying to remember and then repeated the same advice about the gangsters coming after me. His final words were "Son, I love you. Remember it is all about choices. Make good choices."

We drove home in silence. He went home to be with his Lord that night. It tore a hole in my heart that would take a long, long time to scab over. It never fully healed, but one thing I was sure that night, he heard His Lord say, *Welcome home, my good and faithful servant.*

I took solace in the fact that the year before he died, I gave him something to be proud of me for. I had applied to the University of Detroit. At the time, the university was the second most prestigious college in Michigan, also very expensive. I did not know what I was thinking. We did not have two nickels to rub together. My grades in high school were not that great either. The guidance counselor, Miss Gibson, thought so little of me that she would not even part with one of her two copies of applications to the U of D. "Go to a community college for a couple of years, get your grades up, and try applying then." Another teacher, Miss Gutow, encouraged me to believe in myself and go for it. I decided to go for it anyway, against the odds. I drove to the university to pick up an application form, filled it out, and sent it in.

I was working several jobs until all hours of the night and going to school during the day. One Thursday night, I got home after one in the morning. There was a letter on my dresser from the University of Detroit. They had accepted me. My joy was instantly crushed with the thought that they must have made a mistake and sent it to the wrong guy. With the confusion over my last name, it would not have been the first time. I did not say anything to my family because I could not bear to disappoint my dad. The next day, I came home late again to another letter on my dresser. My heart sunk, I was sure they made a mistake and would rescind their offer. I was wrong. This letter was from the president of the university, Father Malcom Carron, saying that I was one of five graduating seniors he would most like see attend the University of Detroit next fall. I was in shock. Now I knew they had the wrong guy, and this was going to blow up when they found their mistake. This kind of good news does not happen to a guy like me.

The following Saturday morning was the first time I saw my dad in days. I sat at the kitchen table, with him debating whether to say anything to him. The disappointment would kill him when they found out they had the wrong guy. After the first pot of coffee, the mailman delivered another letter. I was so glad I had not told him anything. I thought of just taking the letters out back to burn them but went into my bedroom to open the letter in private, I screamed. It was a full ride scholarship to the University of Detroit. Everyone came running. I showed them all the letters. Except for the death of his mother, my grandmother, and the wedding day of my sister Maryjo, I had never seen my dad cry before. He just hugged me and hugged me with tears of joy running down our faces. His boy was going to make it!

3

The Boy Goes to College and Still Wants to be a Gangster

I barely graduated from high school in the spring of 1971. Two weeks before graduation, my dad had another heart attack. After working a double shift the night before, I pulled into the parking lot at school. When I got out of my car, I threw my cigarette butt on the pavement and stepped on it (I was a smoker by my eighth birthday.). A retired ROTC major who was a hall monitor approached me. The Vietnam war was going on hot and heavy at this time and he must have felt like I disrespected him or something. He made the mistake of grabbing me and shoving me against my car. Now I disrespected him. He marched me down to the Principal's office. On the way, he told me that he was going to have me suspended and I would not be able to graduate with my class. I threatened his wellbeing and his life. It seemed to me, my dad was living to see me graduate. and this would crush him.

The assistant principal saw us coming and intervened. He told the major he would take it from here. I went into his office. I had been this assistant principal's bookie for the last three years. We were friends. Even though I had plenty of dirt on him, I would never have used it. He was a good guy. He arranged for me to do twenty hours of work detail after school with the janitors instead of being suspended. My job after school with the janitors was hanging out, smoking, and drinking beer. The irony was not lost on me. But hey, in the end, my dad got out to see me graduate and get my diploma. It was a big deal.

That fall, I started at the U of D. My first class was a political science class. I thought that because I liked to talk, I might make a good politician. I was clueless. There were as many kids in this class as there were in my entire graduating class at high school. I made friends with guys that I would stay friends with for life.

Not that there was a choice, because personal computers had not been invented then, but I could never understand the concept of an online college education. The most important part of college in my opinion is the people you meet, the social skills you develop, and the lifelong friendships you create. The piece of paper you get in the end, the diploma, will introduce you in the workforce, but the relationships you make during those formidable years will help define who you really are and what type of people you will have in your life forever.

That very first day in that very first class, I ran into one of two guys I knew from my neighborhood. His name was John. He was also an Italian kid. They called him Chinky. Everybody had a nickname back then. He hated it. I only called him that when I wanted to piss him off. I went to grade school with him until he transferred to a Catholic boys' high school. We had lost touch but now were reunited. Chinky was a piece of work. He knew everybody and had a memory like none I ever knew. That was his gift. He introduced me to a guy. I liked most everybody I met, and I considered myself to be a pretty likable guy. This guy and I could not stand each other immediately. I later asked Chinky what he saw in the arrogant clown named Chris. He was a half Syrian and half Italian so I guess he was at least half okay.

Chinky continued to introduce me to a bunch of guys. Mostly East Side Detroit ethnic guys. Italian, Syrian wannabe gangster types and just for balance he introduced me to a bunch of brainy guys who were in a professional business fraternity Alpha Kappa Psi. Chris was one of the guys in the fraternity, but he wasn't too brainy though. Chinky thought we ought to join the fraternity. The catch was you needed to be in the school of business to join. Chinky convinced me to give up on my idea of going into politics. I admit, it didn't take much convincing. He just said, "Forget it, that politics crap, if we go into this business school, we can hang with all these brainiacs, go into business with them, and make a killing. If you want, you can buy all the politicians you want." It sounded logical to me. We changed majors to business that day and joined our new friends. Chris kind of sponsored me, and we have been lifelong best friends ever since.

I was in one of my classes when a whole bunch of my new fraternity brothers came rushing over and told me that they had just come from their marketing class and that I needed to come with them to that class the next day. They were very excited but would not tell me anything else, so the next day, I accompanied them to Mr. Pradnicki's Marketing 101 class. One of the guys asked Mr. Pradnicki to repeat what he was talking about the previous day. He asked why. They said that they had brought a friend to the class, and I needed to hear what was said yesterday. They told him my name. There was a gasp by the other classmates, and Mr. Pradnicki started talking about customer service, and he told a story about the best marketing and merchandising man he had ever met. The Pradnicki family owned five grocery stores in the Metro Detroit Area, and he had told the class they could learn all they needed to learn about marketing and merchandising by spending just one day working with a Stroh Beer Delivery man whose name was Al Dimercurio, my father. Mr. Pradnicki could not believe that I was the son of this man. I was the proudest guy on the planet. Tears of joy streamed down my face. I rushed home to tell my dad that he, too, had made it to collage. I was right all along. He was the best, and now they were teaching about how great he was at the university. Who was to know what awaited us right around the corner? But for this day, we were on top of the world. Back to Chinky, remember I said he knew everyone? Unfortunately, that was true. He knew every gangster type in the city, bosses, sons of bosses, and friends of bosses as well as where they lived and what racket they were into. He also knew all the bookies, hustlers they had their hooks into, and all the gangster wannabes. I met them all. I was invited to all their events, card parties, crap games, and bachelor parties. The best was when they were throwing a going away party for one of the boys going to college. I was so green in those days. I remember seeing the smile on one of the bosses' face when I asked him what college the guest of honor was going to. He told me the University of Jackson, which was Jackson State Prison. He would be back out seven to fifteen years, depending on good behavior. Everyone had a good laugh at my expense. I tried not to ask too many questions after that. I found out there were good and bad in all types of people, whether gangsters, cops, politicians, businessmen, professors, and even priests and pastors. The pledge period began for AKPSI fraternity shortly after I transferred to the school of business. There were about twelve pledges in my class. Many of us have stayed friends now for over forty-five years. My job in the pledge class was to organize, plan, and implement the year's public service event. I knew little about public service or organizing. I would have considered it a public service to take out a bad guy or a corrupt cop but hey, I was trying to turn over a new leaf so what the hell. I do not know how it happened or how I found out about this place, but it changed my life direction.

I found myself at the Healy Center for children in Southwest Detroit. It was an orphanage. I was talking to the directors about how my fraternity could help the children. Easter was coming up and the kids had nothing to look forward to. I sprang into action. I was good at delegating so I put a team together. I went to my old stand-bys first, my sisters Julee Ann and MaryJo. Next were my cousins, the pledge class, and even some guys from the fraternity and their *tomadas* (girlfriends). We went to all the stores that everyone frequented. My instructions to my team was to lean on the owners and managers and make them drop down "donate" their leftover candy, toys, games, and stuffed animals for Easter. We filled up our entire basement with goodies for the kids, including thousands of plastic Easter eggs that my sisters filled with candy.

The mood at the orphanage was somber when we got there that Saturday morning. The children had a bad week, we were told, thinking the Easter Bunny missed them because after all nobody wanted them, not even him. To be honest, I think the staff was getting depressed too, thinking we had dropped the ball and forgotten about them. I guess that was what they were used to. Car after car, loaded with college kids, began showing up with tons of goodies, food, and drinks. We had the best Easter egg hunt. The sounds of kids squealing with joy as they ran around the playground lifted our hearts. Laughter and tears filled the place with the thought that even for just one day, we made a difference in the lives of these children. Truth be told, it was them that had made a difference in our lives. A huge difference. I learned right there:

You cannot outgive God.

There were two little kids in there who seemed to be ostracized by the other children. They were shaking in fear and seemed so sad. I wanted to fix it. One of the stores donated two huge, almost life-size Easter baskets loaded with candy, coloring books, and giant stuffed Easter bunnies. These baskets had to be five feet tall and wrapped in colorful cellophane. I arranged before the Easter egg hunt that whomever "found" the two eggs with the special tokens in them would win these baskets. Guess who found the two special eggs? Everybody wanted to be their new best friends. Problem solved, even if for only that day. Oh, how I wanted to bring these two kids home with me to love them, provide for them, and protect them. It was right then that I decided I wanted kids in my life. I asked God in my unique way to give me children, lots of children. I did not even think at the time that a wife was all that necessary. *I could handle it alone,* I thought. As you will later see, this God we serve has His own ideas and, I would find out, quite a sense of humor.

4

God Gives Me an Angel

I was living the dream and making new friends. My world was growing wider and wider every day. I was a college boy and a gangster. I was partying every night, free as a bird. There were girls everywhere. I was on top of the world...until my world came tumbling down.

Alphonse Dimercurio—my dad, my mentor, my role model, and my everything—went home to be with His Lord. I cursed the Lord that day and for many days that followed. How could God let this happen? I was just getting to know my dad as a man. This God, his God, would take him away from me. I wanted no part of this God. I hated Him. However, I learned something in the next three days after his death. I learned that God really did exist and that my father was with him. When I saw my dad laid out in the coffin, I knew it was no longer my dad. This was nothing more than the shell he had occupied while he was here on earth. My dad was so much more than this shell. He was so full of life. He radiated love. His personality was so big. Where had all that gone? It was certainly not laying there in the box.

The priest said it was written in the Bible, "To be absent from the body is to be present with the Lord." He backed that up with the story about Jesus hanging on the cross between two thieves when one thief was taunting Jesus and the other one said something like, "Shut up, fool! We deserve what we are getting. This man has done no wrong." Then turning to Jesus, he said, "Remember me, Master." Jesus replied, "Because of your belief, this day, you shall be with me in paradise." Surly that is where my father's spirt was.

We all fell into a deep depression. I just knew we were going to lose my mother too. No one could stop crying. Everything he said to me, warned me of, and made me promise him had been ingrained in my very soul, but now they were just rattling around in my brain. I was so confused. I felt like the weight of the world was on my shoulders. We all did. He instructed us all to stay together. "Nothing can break you if you stay together. If you go off one by one," he would say, illustrating by separating his fingers on his hand, "the world and the devil will break you off like a little limb on a tree. Making a fist, he would slam it down on the table, "But if you stay together, no one can break you. Treat your mother like a queen. You are the man of the house now, take care of your sisters, and get an education. If you want to sleep at night don't hook up with the gangsters. Family is everything."

His family, brothers, and sisters bailed on us first. We saw them almost every week my entire life, but they stopped coming around after his passing. They eventually stopped inviting us for holidays, saying it was just too hard on them to see us without their brother. "Choices, make good choices Frank. You are where you are because of the choices you make. If you do not like where you are, make better choices."

Well, it was time for me to make some choices. I cut myself off from his brothers and sisters. I was so angry, I could not even be polite to them. That choice would have really disappointed him. He loved them so much. The next choice would have killed him if he were still alive. I dropped out of school. I started my first business, an auto reconditioning business. My family was broke. I was on a full scholarship, but my brain was fried. *I could not even think straight*, I reasoned. I cannot pay bills with scholarship papers. I was already breaking my promise to him to get an education. He broke the deal first, he left.

He had not been gone for a month when the mobsters were lining up to recruit me. They hung out at my reconditioning shop, gambling and whoring around. They started bringing in some heavy hitters. This was at the time when Jimmy Hoffa disappeared. We cleaned the cars of all these guys every week. The Mercury that was allegedly used to pick up Jimmy Hoffa at the infamous Markus Red Fox Restaurant in Bloomfield Hills, Michigan, was cleaned in my shop the day before Jimmy took his last ride. The guys will remain anonymous because I still like breathing. Sometimes silence is golden. Anyhow, it was reported that these same guys had taken this Mercury to a car wash on the west side of Detroit because the owner of the car told the feds he got blood in his truck from transporting a fish. One thing I know for sure, no fish had ever been in that vehicle. Two days before, that truck was loaded with weapons that could have started a small war. Unfortunately, the owner of that car wash ended up dead that week. I was always thankful that car got washed on the other side of town that fateful day. God rest his soul. Enough said on that topic.

Several years of frustration followed. My career choices were narrowing as a bookie, head buster, or businessman for the bosses. The choices were looking bleak. My father's words were haunting me from the grave.

Who are you going to serve? It is all about choices.
My choices sucked.

In the summer of 1975, I went to lunch one day with one of my other best friends and now partner in the auto reconditioning shop, Bob Rashid. We went to a Clock Restaurant and we ran into his future sister-in-law, Julie. She was supposed to meet a friend who did not show up for some reason, so we joined her for lunch. She was beautiful. Bob shocked us both when he took out a box with an engagement ring and told us he was going to propose to Julie's sister that night. We were so happy for them. That night when I went to bed, I began a conversation with God whom I had not talked to in a long time. I asked him when will I meet the women that I would marry. Up until then, the girls that I was seeing, well let's just say they were not the marrying type. I began to bargain with the Lord (after all everything was a negotiation wasn't it). "I could change. I can be a good man. A good provider. Couldn't you just please give me a glimpse of my future bride?" I asked. *Oh, what's the use!* I drifted off to sleep thinking of the day's events, including lunch with Bob and Julie. *When will you ever answer me, God?*

Bob and Nancy, his future bride, asked me to be an usher in their wedding that would take place the next year. They also asked Nancy's sister, Julie. At the reception of their wedding, I asked Julie to dance with me. While dancing, I remarked to Julie, holding her close to me, that she seemed to fit. She agreed. A couple of days later, after getting approval from her father (I was old school in some ways), I asked Julie to go out with me. We went out to dinner the following Saturday. At the end of a beautiful evening, while sitting in my car, Julie started saying my last name over and over and then added her first name to my last, Julie Dimercurio. I said it has a nice ring to it. She agreed. I asked her right then and there if she would like to be my bride. She said yes on our very first date. Sometimes you just know that you know. We were made for each other.

When my future father-in-law saw that we were getting awfully close to each other, more like inseparable, he said, "Hey, you guys better slow down! I have not even paid off the last wedding yet. I need at least…a week. I apologized and said, "I am sorry, sir. It is too late." I then asked him for Julie's hand in marriage. To say that he was shocked would be putting it mildly. Happy, but shocked. We were married a few months later.

God granted my wish. The girl I had fallen asleep dreaming about nearly two years before became my bride. It was the same night that I started talking to the Lord again and asked Him for a vision of her. He had given me the vision that night, and now He gave me an angel.

Julie in my Mind God Sends an Angel.

5

Living with Cystic Fibrosis

This union with Julie was not without its challenges. Julie had cystic fibrosis, a disease that severely limited her ability to breathe. She lost several siblings to this disease, but she was a fighter. She loved her Lord and never had a moment of self-pity in her entire life. She would care for other people who felt like they were dying when all they had was a simple cold or council a friend or relative who were trying to deal with their problems that seemed so trivial to me compared to hers.

Many people objected to me marrying Julie. Some well-meaning friends tried to stop me by saying, "You don't understand, she is going to die!" My response to all of them was the same, "Then I have some bad news for you. We are all going to die, even Jesus died, and so will you and I." I just figured better one day in His or Her court than a thousand elsewhere.

Cystic Fibrosis is a childhood genetic disease that attacks the lungs, digestive tract, and pancreas. It is not contagious so you cannot catch it. You are born with it and it usually results in a shortened life span. Back in the 1960's and 1970's, very few children would reach their teenage years, much less live long enough to get married. Julie and I were one of the first couples to ever marry. Julie was nineteen at the time of our wedding. I was twenty-three. The Cystic Fibrosis Foundation asked us to be their representatives to encourage other CF patients and give some hope to their families. We became surrounded by photographers, television reporters, and radio personalities doing public service announcements. Speaking engagements at most CF fundraising events became very routine. I even played Santa Clause for these events and many other organizations for forty years.

Treatments for CF patients at that time were very primitive at best. Eating was hard enough, but with every meal, Julie would have to take handfuls of enzymes to help her digest her food. More often than not, she would "lose her cookies," as she would call it. Julie was extremely photogenic. She had a smile that was infectious. Her inner beauty was instantly apparent. The phrase "To know her was to love her" was her epitaph. Christ shined through this girl in everything she did. She had a very personal relationship with the Lord, and she shared it everywhere she went. Me, on the other hand...well, let's just say, this was a classic beauty-and-the-beast story. I was a walking, talking contradiction of good and evil. My friends and family adored me. I was fiercely loyal and dependable. My enemies and the enemies of my friends and family feared me like I was the plague.

Julie was my Achilles' heel. To say I was protective would have been an immense understatement. She was off-limits to anyone who would cause her unhappiness or, God forbid, pain. Some of the worst offenders were the press corps with their jaded, brainless, heartless, and cruel reporters. It was bad enough that when Julie was giving interviews right from her hospital bed, they would need to twist her words, leave out all references to her God, and then have the audacity to photograph her when she was at the sickest, maybe even throwing up. It cost them a few cameras as I threatened to feed what was left of these cameras to them. When they would lead off their story with a statement saying that she was dying from cystic fibrosis, she would correct them and kindly say, "Oh no, I am not dying from CF. I am living with it." We came to expect this type of behavior from these predators. What I could never prepare for was the cruelty of the so-called Christians at her church, the church she loved and put so much faith in.

Julie coughed constantly, trying to expel the mucus buildup from her lungs so she could breathe. In no way was anyone in danger of catching anything, but the ignorant "church people" would look at her with such distain. The old ladies would tell her to go home where she belonged or that she was being so selfish being there, infecting all of the elderly holy people. We even had a priest tell us that she had no place in "their" church. I must admit that I have committed more sins in church than I ever did on the streets. I was no angel. I offered to "baptize" this *holy man* in a way he would have never imagined. I extended the offer to his precious congregation as well. Little did they know, Julie was praying for them. In the words uttered by Jesus Himself, she repeated, "Father, forgive them, they no not what they do." Nothing changed in the past two thousand years, I surmised. I cannot even imagine what she was praying for me. Whatever it was, it was not working at the time…or was it.

With a sick wife and no job, (I had sold my businesses to get a more stable job with benefits. I got laid off after eighty-nine days.) I would turn to God again. We headed to Quebec, Canada. I told myself this was for Julie. What I did not know was the Holy Spirit was calling me. The Basilica of Sainte-Anne-de-Beaupré is a Catholic church in Quebec, Canada, which has an incredibly special place in my family's history. We received many answered prayers there in the past. Just before my father died, my parents, aunt and uncle went to Saint Anne's on a pilgrimage. One day, my dad had a massive heart attack on a bench just outside the entrance to the cathedral. We got the call late one afternoon that our father was not expected to live much longer. I went into full-blown panic mode. I needed to be with my parents to protect them and fix things. My sister Maryjo, who lived only a mile from us and just had her third baby girl that January, came over to tell my sister Julee Ann and me what had happened. Mom called back later that night to give us an update. "Like hell!" I said. "I'm leaving right now." It is a thirteen-hour ride. I would be there by morning if I left right away. A fight broke out between the three of us on what we should do. I conceded that I would wait until Mom called back. Then I was gone.

When she called, she was shaking so badly, she could barely talk. He was still alive, and they had taken him to a larger hospital in Quebec City. She told me to stay put for the time being. She cried even harder and put my uncle Tony on the phone He ordered me to wait for his call before I left. He said he had things covered for now. He would need me to get some things together and keep a cool head. He knew I was a hot head. Uncle Tony was not a boss, but he was very connected, and I trusted him. He was the husband of my mother's sister, Josie. I worked for him as a small-time bookie. It was decided that my sister Julee Ann and I would come up there in two days when my aunt and uncle would come home. Maryjo had to stay back and take care of the babies.

My mom made us promise to stop for the night somewhere along the way because she did not want us driving at night. We said okay, but we both knew that was not going to happen. We stopped to get something to eat, even though neither one of us were hungry. When we came out of the restaurant, five or six guys were all around my car, trying to steal the tires. I walked my sister to the car as they slowly backed away. I got her inside the car and told her not to move no matter what. I opened my trunk where I had the only weapon I could bring with me across the border, an old axe handle that I still carry with me to this day. It was a remarkably effective tool. I went after them like a mad man and would have killed them if I caught the degenerates. I returned to the car. We would not be stopping again.

Everyone was so glad when we arrived. Dad was in a semicoma. My aunt and uncle left, I felt so abandoned in a foreign nation where next to no one even spoke our language. They spoke our language but would not speak it to us and the only French I could speak; you would not want to use it for general conversation or to go to Sunday services. The only nice people I found were the owners of this little junkie motel where we all crammed into. The others were terrible to us. The French Canadians only hated one thing more than Canadians from Ontario who spoke English, that would be Americans. I wanted to start World War III. All I had in my heart was anger and distain for all Canadians from that time on. How could they be so cruel to human beings, fellow Christian human beings?

We sat at his bedside for weeks. When he came out of the coma, he was so glad to see us. He would talk for hours, trying to prepare us for a life without him. How do you prepare for the unthinkable? He told us in minute detail how beautiful St. Anne's Cathedral is. He did not know that we had been there already. It was twenty or thirty miles away. I would take my mom there most nights to pray after visiting hours were over. Dad told us how huge and ornate it was and how he felt so close to God inside that building. He even described the musty smells of old braces, crutches, and walking sticks that adorned the giant spires near the entrance as well as how many altars they have. "You must see it, Frank. It is amazing." He forgot that I told him I had been there many times. The only problem was, my dad never stepped foot in the basilica. He had collapsed while walking from the parking lot to the building and ended up on a bench outside the side entrance where the EMS service picked him up and performed CPR on him before transporting him to the hospital. When I told him this, he said that was ridiculous and again described everything inside with even more detail. Somehow, someway, he had been in that church.

I asked God to help me get him home. He wanted to see his grandchildren again and to die on American soil. After several weeks, the doctors told us they were amazed that his heart was functioning at all, in as bad a shape it was in, they let us take him home with a bottle of aspirin. He died ten days later after seeing all his loved ones. How great is this God?

Fast-forward to years later, here I was with no job, a sick wife, and huge medicals bills. I was too proud to ask for help. I had a lukewarm faith on my best days. It was not that I ever denied God existed, I was always pissed off at him. I blamed him for everything. So what was I to do? Considering myself very resourceful, I devised a foolproof plan. It was time to put the plan into action.

As I have mentioned before, I am of Italian descent, a second-generation American. We have our own way of thinking. There are some things we value more than life itself. It is our code of honor. Our mothers are sacred to us. We live for their approval. However, most times, our mothers are so afraid of us getting hurt or, God forbid, getting into an accident and had to be rushed to the hospital with dirty underwear on. What would the nurses think? That you have a *puttana* for a mother? How could you bring shame on the family this way? So, given that our mothers would say no to "everything," it was always better to go to *nonna* (Italian for grandma). She had this kind of power. She could ask her grandchildren to do anything, and it would be done. Nothing on heaven or earth outranked *nonna*. Her word was final. Now I deduced that if my *nonna* had this much power over me and the family, how much more leverage would Jesus's grandmother have over Him? I was always working the angles and Saint. Anne was the Virgin Mary's mother, Jesus's grandmother. Ha-ha, I had figured it out. I needed a miracle, and I would just go ask her to ask her grandson for one.

6

On Our Way to Hear from God

We drove to Saint Anne's on a Tuesday afternoon. The entire place was empty. That was surreal. I knelt at the statue of Saint Anne with Julie at my side. We began to pray and talk to the saint and Jesus. I had never prayed like this before. I begged Him for help and then I made Him a promise. Why this promise, why this way, I will never know. I said, "Lord, you have given me this girl, your child. I swear an oath to you this day if it be your will I will love her, cherish her, care for her, and provide for her, if it be seven days, seven months, or seven years." Why was this? Why didn't I ask for more time? What was I thinking?

While I was deep in prayer, Julie got up, started yelling, and ran back toward the entrance. About halfway down the aisle, she stopped and began to projectile vomit. The puke came out like a power hose that was turned on. Wave after wave of thick, mucus-filled vomit poured out of her. I rushed to her side and screamed for help. There was no one around to help us. As she continued to throw up, I ran to the back of the vacant building and saw a small office labeled "Janitor" on the door. I pounded on the door.

A short monk in a brown robe with a rope tied around his waist said in perfect English that his name was Brother Dominic. I told him what was happening to Julie. He smiled at me and said, "Jesus has heard your prayer, my son." He then followed after me with a rolling cart filled with sawdust. The marble floor of the surrounding area was filled with vomit, eerily illuminated by an unknown source.

Brother Dominic tossed the sawdust over it. As he swept the floor, the light disappeared.

I picked Julie up, carried her to the car, and drove her to our motel room. She said she was breathing normally for the very first time in her life. She slept peacefully in my arms as I cried tears of joy throughout the night. The following morning, we realized that we had not even thanked Brother Dominic. We got dressed and went back to the Saint Anne's. The place was bustling with people. Groups of all sizes had come in buses and filled the parking lot. I began asking to speak to someone who spoke English and was sent to an office, way behind the main altar. We were welcomed by the head priest and administrator of the church. I told him of our experience the day before and asked him if he could get Brother Dominic so we could thank him properly. With a peculiar look on his face, he asked me to describe Brother Dominic. I did. Then he told us that there was no Brother Dominic or any other brother who worked there yesterday. He added that in all his years as the administrator, this was the third time there was a sighting of a man dressed in monk's clothing that reportedly had been seen there, but it was the very first time that the monk had given anyone his name.

I was a skeptical guy up until this point in my life, but even I could not deny what we just witnessed and the powerful results of our prayers instantly answered. There was a God, and He loved me.

Julie at St. Ann's Falls On our way to hear from God

7

Seven Years of Bliss

Some people consider having long life the goal. I happen to know people who lived well into their eighties, nineties, and some have made it over a hundred years old with marriages that have lasted sixty or seventy years. Some were great. Then there are others you have to ask yourself, *Why? What for?* Lives with no purpose. Dead marriages that look like two enemies just caught up in a game of stare down waiting to outlast the other partner, if only out of spite. God gave us just over seven years. We shared more love, happiness, joy, sorrow, grief, pain, and fulfillment in those seven years than most couples get to have in seventy years. As the song says, "Better is one day in His courts (or in this case, *her* court) than a thousand elsewhere."

About three years into our marriage, I was working as a delivery driver for Pepsi. While making my first delivery of the day, tragedy struck. I ripped a muscle in my shoulder and neck area. I was in terrible pain. The doctors said that because of the location of the tear, it could take as long as three years with rehab to heal. Until then, I may never be able to lift that kind of heavy weights again. I was devastated. I blamed God again. "Can't you cut me a little slack?" I asked Him. "Don't you remember our deal?" What was I going to do? How was I going to provide for her? My dad's words came back like a sledgehammer. "Son, develop you brain. If all you have is your brawn, when that goes, you will have nothing to fall back on."

The night before this happened, I was out with a buddy of mine who was a crazy driver. He was rear-ended, which snapped my head backward. Not giving it a second thought, I just got up and went to work the following morning. The tear may have happened in the car accident, but lifting those cases sure finished it off. I called my insurance company to see if I had any coverage that could at least help wave my insurance payments. The agent said, "I am sorry, sir. You have no such coverage, however, you have a work-loss benefit."

"What is that?" I asked.

"Oh, the company will pay you ninety-five percent of your nontaxable pay for the next three years, if you are off that long." Praise God! What a gift from God it was.

Julie, concerned about my mental health and knowing about the promise I had made to my father about getting my degree, encouraged me to go back to U of D and finish my degree. I reluctantly agreed, but because I did not want her to be alone at night, I decided to go back to day school.

On my first day, I went in early to pay a visit to my old buddy, the dean of the business school. When I walked into his office, he stared at me as if I was a ghost. He hung his head and playfully started banging his head on his desk. He said he had seen my name on his forms and thought it had to be a mistake. His luck could not be that bad. The first time I was there six years ago, I was the student president, of the Business School and I had drove him nuts. We laughed. I left his office and went to my first class, freshman English, which I skipped my first time around. As I entered the classroom a couple of minutes late, the eighteen-year-old kids all straightened up and ceased talking. All eyes were on me, the old man who just entered the room. *Oh no, what have I gotten myself into!* I looked around the room. There was no teacher present. I just announced that I did not feel up to it this today, dismissed the class, and then I walked out of the room. Apparently, they all followed, with a couple of exceptions. When the real professor showed up to his almost empty classroom, he was not amused.

Two days later, he was there early, lying in wait for the old man student. He hated me. Every paper I turned in, he would pick apart and give me horrible grades. One day, he gave us an assignment to write a descriptive paper about a family heirloom. I had to ask one of the kids what an heirloom was. I was told it was something that had been in your family for generations. I had worn hand-me-downs most of my life so I did not know anything about heirlooms. I made up a story about my great-great-grandfather in Italy who had this sawed-off shotgun called a *lupara* (meaning, wolf killer). I wrote about how he had to deal with people who would unjustly cause pain on anyone in our family since the cops were all crooked. My great-great-grandfather would have to take his *lupara* and shoot down the bullies of his time and get rid of the bodies. Then he passed this shotgun down to several generations of my family, and now it was mine. The story scared the hell out of this professor. He gave me an *A minus* on it. It was the first ever *A* in that class. I figured I would push my luck. After the class, I went up to him and asked, "Why the minus?" He quickly looked the paper over and changed my grade to an *A*. He also ended up given me an *A* for my semester grade. He now wanted to be my new best friend.

Over the next two years, I completed all my classes and received a BS degree in business administration with a minor in psychology with a special emphasis on the BS. At the dean's insistence, I walked on commencement day wearing a cap and gown. He handed me my diploma in front of thousands in attendance, including my wife, my mother, both sisters, and my brother-in-law. Somewhere in that room, I am sure the spirit of my dad was there too. *I had kept my promise, Dad.*

Nearing the end of the seven years, Julie asked me for something. She had only asked me for one other thing in those seven years. It was a little trinket memento. We had came home from a little trip to upper Michigan' and when we got home, she remarked that she knew we were really low on money, she didn't bother to ask me for a few bucks to buy this trinket that she really admired. The next weekend, we drove back up there against her objections to buy that trinket. She treasured it. What she asked for now was a little more difficult.

As she was getting sicker, her hospital stays were getting longer. One day at home, feeling a little better, she said she always had wanted to go to SeaWorld in Florida to kiss Shamu the whale. I joked, asking her, "Why do you need to kiss that whale when you have me right here? After all, I weighed over three hundred pounds!" She laughed but said she had always wanted to kiss Shamu. So I booked the flights. We could not afford it, but I could never say no to her. We arrived in Orlando, rented a car, and headed to our hotel room. Something terrible happened. Julie's breathing had taken an awfully bad turn for the worst. The humidity was also complicating things. Through a forced smile, she said she would be all right and insisted in going to SeaWorld. I was sweating bullets, not knowing what to do. She objected to going to the hospital because she said they would kill her at a strange hospital not knowing her history. She added that as soon as we went to SeaWorld, she would let me call her doctor back home and get some directions. Off to SeaWorld we went. I insisted on getting her a wheelchair and pushed her around the park. She was so happy, struggling but happy. I wheeled her into an attraction that would take about half an hour in the air conditioning and told her I would be right back.

I asked to speak to a manager, and they sent out some assistant manager. I tried to explain to him about Julie's wish to kiss Shamu. He laughed at me and said that was impossible. The people who were called up during the performance were all corporate donors and their family and friends. Even arrangements for them had to be made months in advance. I pleaded with him, telling him of our dire circumstances, to no avail. That is when the other side of me showed up once again, a side I thought I had buried and was gone forever. I "firmly" put my hand on this guy's shoulder and told him that my problem had now become his problem, that he could solve this problem quickly and uneventfully or he was going to have a huge dead fish floating in that aquarium for all his corporate donors to see. He turned white as a sheet and hurried off. I fully expected to be arrested, but he returned very soon with the general manager.

Within an hour, with cooler heads prevailing, Julie unknowing that any of this drama had transpired was shocked when the announcer at the aquarium exhibit announced that Shamu had a special request. He had his eye on a pretty lady in the stands and wanted to give her a kiss. "Would Julie Dimercurio please come up to the podium?" I wheeled her down there. The trainer had the whale come right out of the water, up on the platform, and into the outstretched arms of Julie. She hugged him and gave him a big kiss that was caught on a Polaroid camera. She was so happy. I was so relieved.

Julie and Frank after Shamoo's Kiss

8

The End of the World as I Knew It

After Julie's date with Shamu, I called her doctor and told him what had happened. He ordered me to take her to a hospital immediately. He rightfully guessed that Julie's lung had collapsed, possibly from the air pressure in the cabin of the plane on the way to Florida. Julie refused to go to the hospital. After much arguing with the doctor, he arranged for us to pick up some oxygen tanks but insisted that under no condition was she to get on an airplane. He made me promise that if her oxygen level sank below a certain point, I would overrule her and get her to an emergency room. I called the Alamo car rental place to tell them that I was taking their car to Detroit. They had a fit and told me that car could not leave the state. I said it was not a debate. I just wanted them to know where they could pick up their car. We drove straight though for the next twenty-plus hours to Bon Secours Hospital in Grosse Pointe, Michigan. Julie would never leave the hospital again in her earthly body.

The next three months were brutal. The treatments were less and less effective. Her body was breaking down. I stayed by her side the entire time. The hospital staff was wonderful. Her lifelong doctor and his students, not so much. The doctor informed us that his wife booked an extended Mediterranean cruise so he would be gone for six weeks. Julie never knew another doctor. Her doctor even delivered her when she was born. I saw the disappointment in her eyes and glimpsed what might have been fear. His replacement came into our room to do rounds with his entourage of students. He asked one of his students to give a report. This idiot gave a rundown of Julie's

40

history like we were not even there. The doctor asked the prognosis and said in medical jargon that her organs were shutting down and her lungs were filling with fluid. She had less than three weeks to live. They turned and walked out of the room. It was the first time anyone had ever put it into words.

I sat there in shock. Julie's mom was there with tears streaming down her face.

Julie tried to comfort her, "It will be all right, Mom. I can handle this."

My knees turned to jelly. I could not even stand up. When I did, I said I would be right back. I left the room as rage filled my body. I ran down the hallway and caught up with the doctors. It took five guys to pull me off this punk. How dare he be so insensitive? I fired them and warned them to never come in that room again. The nursing staff tried to explain to me that this is why they call it the "practice of medicine." I suggested they should try to *master* the practice of humanity first before they tried the field of medicine.

The following Saturday, we almost lost her. They called a code. After what seemed like forever, they resuscitated her. The doctor who rescued her left me a business card that I slipped into my pocket. He said to give him a call if I ever needed help. Her mother was holding her. With a smile, Julie told her mother that her Mimi and Opa (grandma and grandpa) were with her. She described them in detail and told her mother they have a message for her. Julie had never met her grandparents. They died before she was born. Her mother asked her why she did not just go with them. Her gaze turned to me and she said, "Because Frank is not ready yet."

In the next seven days and nights, I pleaded with Julie not to leave me. I wanted to go with her. I decided that I did not want to live without her. I would take my life after she passed so we could be together. She insisted it could not work that way. If I did that, we would never see each other again. I could not understand all these religious rules. "Why couldn't I just be with you?"

"Because God is not done with you, honey. He has more work for you to do." No truer words were ever spoken—for me, that is.

"But how will I know you are okay?" I asked.

"If there is any way possible, I will send you a signal or come back to let you know," she said.

"But how will I know it is really you?"

"You will know. We have a password. Do not share this with anyone."

I promised I will not.

On the morning of August 10, 1984, my world was changed forever. With her entire family and most of our friends around, Julie looked into my eyes as I held her tightly. Struggling for every breath, she said, "Honey, it is time."

I said, "I know, baby."

She then looked up into what I know was the face of her Lord and said, "Jesus, I am ready!" She laid back and instantly went home with Jesus.

I never felt His presence closer than at that moment in my life. But I was crushed.

9

The Living Dead Years

I never lost faith that God existed. I knew He did, I just hated him. I blamed Him for everything. How could He be so cruel? How could He give me the desires of my heart only to rip it away and leave such a gaping hole? I cursed Him. I even invented words to curse Him. I literally went to war against Him and all His wisdom. "I will show Him!" I declared, calling down more and more misery on myself and anyone else who dared to remain too close to me. Julie's family rejected me. They said it was just too painful to see me and not feel the pain of losing her.

I stayed alone for a year. When I did walk into a room with people, the temperature changed. Laughter and joy stopped dead in its tracks. People began avoiding me like the plague. I did not blame them. I hated being me. I had dug myself a deep, dark, proverbial hole and took up residence at the bottom of it. Only my immediate family and a handful of close friends stayed by my side. There was a price to pay for this loyalty. I dragged them all down with me. A scripture in Proverbs said that a peaceful heart leads to a healthy body. Well, I was anything but peaceful and disease attached me with a vengeance. I began drinking hard liquor every day but not for long. Gout ravaged my body, deforming my joints and forcing me to quit drinking. Heart disease took hold. Evil's presence followed me day and night. Only the prayers of my family and friends kept me alive.

After a particularly bad night, I had enough. I could not take it any longer. I took out my .38 caliber handgun and put the barrel in my mouth. I could feel the battle between good and evil going on in my mind. The evil side kept encouraging me to get it done and just finish it. There was a speck of light still in there. When it began to speak to me, everything stopped. Things stood still for what seemed like hours as the battle raged on. Then I heard, *The second you pull that trigger, what chain of events will you put in place?* "What will it matter? I'll be out of my misery," I replied. *So you think*, the voice in my head argued. *But what will happen to all you leave behind? Are you really that selfish to think that nothing will happen after this action?* "Well, I guess Greg, the neighbor's kid who came by every day, will probably find my body."

This boy was distraught and seeking help in dealing with the death of Julie who he was awfully close to. What would he do? Would he pick up the gun and do the same thing or would he go and break the news to my sister Maryjo? How would she deal with having to tell my mom and sister Julee Ann? This would break them all. How would my buddies feel? Would they think they failed me? Would they have to live the rest of their lives wondering if they could have done more? Would they hate me? I could not blame them if they did. Did I hate all these people so much that I could inflict this kind of pain and misery on all of them? No, I could not do this to them. I loved them more than I hated God and myself.

I put down the gun, broke down, and cried out to the Lord. I then pleaded with Him for help and began the long hard climb out of that dark pit. It was not easy. I slid back more than once on this climb, but I realized that by loving someone and caring for them more than I cared for myself was the key. By giving to others, I would receive all the help I needed. My body started to heal, however, the scars would remain forever. The wear and tear on my body would plagued me all the days of my life. But even this, with God's help, would be overcome.

10

I Have This...No, I Don't

I decided to live again, but where do I go? How do I start? I had been out of the game so long—dating, that is—but I could not stand being alone. It was as if someone had torn me in half. I felt so exposed, so incomplete. It was not like a nice neat cut in half. No, it was more like those strong men who can tear a phone book in half, leaving jagged pieces that just never seemed to line up again. That is what my life felt like. I always had a way to make a bad situation worse. Guys do this kind of thing, we try to fix things on our own. Calling for help is something we rather avoid because we think that vulnerability is a sign of weakness.

Now, just to be fair, let me take a minute to rip on you women. Something has got to be wrong with you. You see a guy who is broken, beat up, barely standing on his own two feet, and you find this attractive? Some pretty boys can pull off getting by in life on their looks alone. Some have a rugged hardness, while some are rather feminine. As for my looks...well, I always thought if you put a dress on me and tried to pass me off as a women, you could take me to the circus and make a fortune showing me as the "Ugliest Woman on the Planet." But as a guy...well, let's just kindly say I have not turned down any offers to be on the cover of *GQ* or *Fitness Today* magazines. To say that women love a challenge is a gross understatement. Everywhere I went, women wanted to "fix" my brokenness. Believe me, they tried to use every tool in their toolbox. The rule books got thrown out the window. Guidelines were all confused and blended. Married women, divorcees, old, young—it did not matter. They all had their own remedies and by God you needed what they had to offer.

"You need to read this book," they would say and then bring it over. "This article in this magazine reminded me of what you are going through," "My cousin, my neighbor, or my girlfriend went through the same kind of loss," or "You need to meet her," and on and on.

"Why do bad things happen to good people?" I heard people say that multiple times? And if I were not screwed up and angry with my feelings already the comments like, "Why would a loving God do something like this to a good guy like you?" As if I should be immune to life itself. I wanted to scream, "I am not a good guy!" I was full of hate, anger, resentment, fear. I could no longer be trusted. Hell, I did not trust myself. I had lost my way. I lost my purpose in life. I would make bad choices one after the other, trying to fill a void I could not possibly fill. I remember ending up in bed with a woman I did not even know. I broke down and sobbed right there in front of her. I felt like I was cheating on my wife when, in fact, I was cheating on myself. Even worse, I was cheating on my God. I wanted to believe this pain was mine at least, that this pain was unique. No other person on the planet could possibly feel as bad as I did. No one could understand. I was even more furious when I learned that not only was all this untrue, books have been written on this topic. People had gotten rich on this topic. Hell, there was an entire industry devoted to burying people like me with information on this topic. I never felt so insignificant in my life.

The phone rang. A woman, the executive director of the Cystic Fibrosis Society, said, "Hi! How are you, Frank? I have been thinking of you for so long. I wanted to call but I just did not want to bother you." I told her I had been meaning to give her a call because I had all these machines we purchased to help Julie breathe that I wanted to donate to another kid who had CF. She heard the pain in my voice. She asked me if I could come out to the CF offices the following day. She wanted me to meet the CF social worker that she thought could help sort out some of my feelings. "No, thank you," I replied. "I can fix myself, but I will come out to bring all the medical supplies and machines."

I had really distanced myself from anything to do with CF. It was just too painful. I could not even stand to hear anyone cough. For seven years, I held these little children in my arms at functions all over the state, performed percussion treatments on them to give their parents a break. I laughed with them. I wiped the tears of the children and parents alike in hospitals, charity events, and way too many funeral homes. "You must go on," I would say. "You have to stay positive for your wife, your other children for your husband. You cannot quit. Never ever quit." I would advise them over and over and over again. Now I was the one who wanted to quit...or so I thought.

I had four nieces at that time, three from my sister Maryjo and one from Julie's sister Nancy. They all could get me to do anything for them. They were so close to their Aunt Julie. The oldest, Lia, was already in high school and the director of a school musical she was doing next Saturday night. They were dedicating the musical to Julie's memory and wanted me there to acknowledge their efforts to collect proceeds from the tickets for the Cystic Fibrosis Foundation. It was pure torture. I never could say no to any of my nieces for anything, and I was not going to start saying no now. So I decided to go.

The next day, I loaded up my car and drove to the foundation's office in Southfield, Michigan. I was ushered into the executive director's office. As we began the small talk, I had my back to the door, quite an unnatural position for me as an Italian. This woman stuck her head in the door and said she will be right back as she had something to finish before she can join us. I glanced over my shoulder when I heard her speak. As I turned to look back at the director, my head just whipped back around to take another look at the hottie in the doorway.

The looks on both these women's faces were of stunned silence. What had just happened? Shortly after, I was introduced to her. "This is Danna. She is our social worker."

I did not know what social workers did, but I instantly decided I needed some social working done. We talked for some time and then Danna and I went to lunch. She told me that she was assigned to go to the musical on Saturday night in my late wife's honor as a representative of the foundation. I asked her if she would like to join me. I would pick her up at her place in Troy. This place would later be renamed Danna Land by my family because of all the time I eventually spent there in the future.

So I picked Danna up on Saturday night. From there, I fell in love instantly all over again. The problem was, it was not with Danna. Oh, Danna was nice, and I liked her. She was hot and I was attracted to her, but I fell in love with Danna's two young daughters. They were incredible. They were smart, funny, and personable. They were instantly taken with me as well. I found my new family, my new home, and my new purpose in life. *I had plenty of love to handle the needs of all three of these wonderful women*, I thought and I dove right into trying to fill up all the holes left in the girls' lives after the ugly divorce of their parents. We were married a little over a year later, a four-ring service at what I called "the Church of What's Happening," a New Age church on the east side of Metro Detroit. To have and to hold, in sickness and in health.

Danna, Frank, and the Girls

This is going to be great, I thought, only to find out after four heartbreaking years that there are some things even I could not fix. This was the first time that I would admit that everyone who knew me saw something that I was totally blind to. My friends, family, and even people I recently met told me different versions, some not proper to repeat here, that I was bat crazy and this marriage had no chance of working. It would be the first time in my life that I was totally wrong. They were totally right, but were they? God sends rainbows even in the worst of storms. I gave everything I had into making our relationship work. I tried to be Mister Everything to everybody.

It was the summer of 1990 now, and things were going downhill in my relationship with Danna. I soon found out that I was extremely sick, and this may have been a contributing factor in the rapid decline of our marriage. Danna and the girls wanted to go out to the movies to see the new box office hit that was just coming out called *Ghost*, starring Patrick Swayze and Demi Moore. I was exhausted but agreed to take them. We arrived at the movie theater over an hour before showtime because all the theaters were selling out fast. When we entered the movie complex, I found out what the girls already knew. They were having a psychic fair in the lobby with tarot-card readers, palm readers, spiritualists, and mediums who could look into your future, playing off what the subject matter of this movie was about. I objected, which led to another fight, but I was outnumbered. I know now what the Bible says about seeking out mediums and that we should not do it, and I do not advise it, but what was to follow was very eerie and unexplainable to me. We stood in line, and at the last minute, the girls took off down the corridor to check out something. Danna followed them, and I found myself standing at the front of the line. This guy, a self-professed medium, motions for me to sit down with him. I was upset. He began by reciting the Lord's Prayer, which I must admit soothed my initial discomfort, and then he looked me over and began to tell me about my relationship and that it was about to be over soon. I asked how he could know this; he said that God had other plans for me. I argued that I did not want my marriage to be over, and that I loved my wife.

He said, "But she does not love you the way you think." He continued. "This is not your first marriage. I see another woman in your
past. What is her name?"

"You're supposed to be the expert. What is her name?" I asked.

He went off into deep thought and said, "I see a J in her name.
June? Judy? No, Julie. That is her name."

The hair on my arms started to stand up on their own. "Julie is
no longer in this world. She has passed to the other side."

"I am starting to see her come into focus. She has long brown
hair, very slim, and very beautiful." He described her perfectly. "She is
glowing and has an aura about her, a very bright aura." He turned his
attention back to me. "Are you familiar with the spirit world?" he asked.

"No," I replied.

He said, "There are ten levels of heaven, and the level you reside
in when you pass to that world is determined by your life on earth.
Your wife, Julie, is from the top levels, either level nine or ten. She is
an incredibly special person." I agreed. "She died from a problem in
her chest or lungs, and she used to cough a lot."

I said, "Yes, she had cystic fibrosis."

"Wait," he said, "she is telling me to tell you something."

All of my defense mechanisms were on full alert now. How is he
doing this? I am looking around the room, trying to figure this out,
when he says, "This doesn't make sense to me, but maybe you will
understand what she is saying. She keeps saying over and over, 'Tell
him this, and he will understand.'" He then proceeded to tell me the
password that Julie and I had set up between us the week before she
died. The password that I have never shared with any other human
being. "Tell him this."

I began to sob. It was her; it had to be her. He then continued
to tell me that she was perfect and very happy; that I would be with
her again, but as she told me on her death bed, she said our Lord had
more work for me to do for him before that time would come.

He told me, "She is saying she has to go now and that she had
a big smile on her face."

I begged him to tell her to stay, but she insisted she had to go
back. I cannot begin to tell you the emotions I was feeling. I had sat

down in that chair less than twenty minutes before, a total skeptic, and now I could not get enough. He turned back to me.

He said, "I see a health problem in you," and he was motioning to his chest area. "You have something wrong going on in your heart area, and if you don't seek help, it could kill you." I almost welcomed the idea of dying right then, and he read my thoughts and said, "It is not wise to ignore the will of God for your life." He continued, "Your current wife will leave you during this time, but I see someone new in your future. You already know this woman, and you will live a long life with this woman, serving the Lord. Her name also starts with a J, but it is not coming to me what her name is."

"Will I have children with this woman?" I asked.

"I see many, many children, but while they are yours, they are not."

What could this mean? I thought. My time was up, and as I rose to leave, Danna and the girls came running up to me, and the look on my face gave me away. I could not share with them what I just experienced, but if any of you have seen the movie *Ghost*, when we went in to view it, this grown man cried through the whole movie.

Within a few weeks, I suffered a heart attack, followed by open-heart surgery, and Danna left me, saying she could not take care of an invalid and raise her two girls and that I would need to figure it out on my own. Six months later, I began dating a longtime customer of mine in my advertising business, named Jinny. We eventually got married, created a successful business, sold it, and moved to Northern Michigan, where we started the Chosen Ranch—a home for children who need a second chance. To date, we have raised many boys and mentored hundreds more. As Julie said through the medium, God had more work for me to do. My wife, who I already knew at the time of the visit with the medium just as a client, her name is Virginia. She goes by Jinny with a J. All the children, while being mine are not mine from a birth relationship, but each of them share a piece of my heart. Now, why do I say not to seek the advice of psychics or mediums and the occult world? Because even in light of everything I experienced that came true in my life, I can see where someone who was unscrupulous could use this knowledge to gain control over your mind and possibly lead you into a very problematic future, maybe even illegal. The other and most important reason is because our Lord tells us in his word not to do it (he does not deny the power exists). He just knows it is not good for us.

Marriage number two had crashed and burned. In some ways, this hurt as bad or worse than the first one. This one was a failure. What had I done so wrong? My self-esteem was shattered, I was sitting on a borrowed, ugly, and uncomfortable orange couch in a two-bedroom apartment that was right across the street from a Meijer store. When I lost my car, as I pessimistically assumed I would, at least I could walk to the store for essentials I bemoaned. What a great outlook on life for a guy who at thirty-eight years old was broke, busted, and disgusted. I was in real estate at this time and I also had a small advertising company that I had to shut down after the heart attack. Both income streams closed faster than a dead fish left out on a hot sunny day. After paying my first and last month's rent, buying a few groceries that consisted of paper plates, plastic utensils, Styrofoam cups, and a big bottle of Motrin, I only had a hundred bucks in my pocket. It was the sum of my life savings, representing my present and future earnings.

But the positive side, I had no debt, having just paid off the last of Danna's credit card. My head sunk into my hands as I openly wept. Tears streamed down my face that I thought I totally expended after Julie passed away. Those tears turned to rage again as I cried out to God. I began cursing Him again. Why did He do this to me again? How bad of a person must I be to be tormented like this over and over? Why was He toying with me like I was a puppet on a string that He would just raise up and then set down in the bottom of that dark pit? *Okay, I hate you, but I have no choice. You win!*

The moments that followed were surreal. I was not sure if they happened in minutes or even hours, but a conversation with God began. I was sure it was all going on in my mind because I did not hear some big, booming voice like Charleston Heston heard in the movie *The Ten Commandments*.

In a soft voice, albeit strong, He said, All right. You and I both know how infrequently we talk. Usually, it is when you have gotten your-

self in trouble. After blaming Me, you call out for an answer or a quick fix. Let's review. There was that day up in Quebec when you cried out to Me for help after your father suffered a massive heart attack. The doctors told you that the damage was so severe that he would never make it home. You pleaded with Me to get him home and let him die with his grandchildren and the rest of your family. I not only did that, but I gave you ten days to spend with him, soaking in all that wisdom he wanted to share with you one last time. You turned your back on Me then. I did not hear from you for years. Then what about the time you went to bed and asked Me to give you a look into your future so that you could see the woman that you one day would marry and call your own. You went to sleep that night thinking and dreaming about the events of the past day and your conversation with your friend Bob's future sister-in-law. You did not know it then, but she was the girl I picked out for you. You were the man she needed. You did not give that night a second thought for a long time. What about the time in Quebec when you took an oath that you would take care of this girl, My girl, for as long as I said whether it be seven days, seven months, or seven years. She was with you for over seven years until she could not bear the suffering of her disease and asked me to take her home. I did the instant she asked. You thanked Me for being merciful then five minutes later, you started hating Me all over again. A couple years later, you asked Me for a family, and I led you to your girls. You did not want Me included in that union too much. It fell apart because of the lack of glue that holds unions together by design, Me.

Hello, anybody awake in there? Now you are sitting here, crying and yelling like a fool, when you know I have been here all along. A year ago, you were complaining about how sick you felt. I sent a doctor who opened up your chest and bypassed the aneurism that was ready to explode and kill you. Now you are on the mend. You are surrounded by friends and family who love you and cannot wait to see you again. You were buried in debt from some very questionable decisions. Now you are debt-free, have two months of rent paid, and even have a spare hundred bucks in your pocket. You were living with a woman you knew did not love you. Now you have this nice bachelor pad and as free as a bird. Son, it is all about choices. You have made so many bad choices. Someday you are going to figure out that these choices should involve Me, but I am afraid that I have to wait a while longer.

My tears dried up instantly. I started to chuckle, then laugh until I was laughing at my own stupidity. Had I finally gone nuts? Could this be happening to me? Was I having a breakdown? How could this be? I just had a conversation with God, and He was making fun of me. It is all in how I look at things

11

The Climb Out of the Black Hole

I spent one year in this apartment. It was crazy. People were coming and going like it had a revolving door. One night, a knock on my door revealed a nurse from a hospital I went to years ago. She was standing there with a brown overnight bag. She walked right in, saying she was on a mission to "fix me." She started setting up candles all over the place and mixed up some concoction for me to drink that was supposed to detox my colon. As I was gagging in the kitchen, she went into the bathroom and slipped into a sheer negligee. Apparently, she felt she needed to clean out my pipes as well. My head was spinning. *What the heck is going on?* A day or two later, my niece asked if she could stay with me because her marriage was falling apart. Her soon-to-be ex had laid his hands on her. She moved in with me the day or two after my night visit from my "nurse". I know Cathy thought I was rescuing her, but it was really her who rescued me from the "nurse." I hung the imaginary "No Vacancy" sign on my door.

Years ago, when I had my advertising and fundraising business, one of my accounts was a small hair salon this woman just opened. She was amazing at doing hair but not so much at running a business. She opened the place on a shoestring and had nothing left over to promote her business. I had a wife, two daughters, a mother, and two sisters who all had to have their hair done on a regular basis. So we cut a deal. I would handle her advertising and she takes care of my family's hair. I was going through a divorce while all the girls are still getting their hair done.

Well anyhow, I needed a haircut, so I went to see Jinny. She heard about our split and was concerned about my health and how I was doing? She had a break in her schedule, so we decided to go down the street to the Big Boy restaurant for coffee… "Just coffee," she said emphatically. She lied. She did not even drink coffee. In fact, she despised coffee. As we sat there, she had this look on her face like she had swallowed a canary when she told me that she just finished my ex's hair. Boy, did she have the dirt on me! She said my ex would come in every couple weeks, just blabbing about what a dirtbag I was. Hell hath no fury like a woman scorned. Since hairdressers are less expensive than physiatrists, Jinny was getting all the goods. She was not held to some kind of oath of silence. We had some good laughs. Then it happened. I swore to myself that since I no longer trusted my own judgment, I would never fall in love again under any circumstances. However, we fell in lust with each other. Jinny was just getting out of a relationship. I guess the stars just aligned. We became great friends with benefits. Both of us were broke so we did not have too many distractions other than work. She had the salon. I went back to being a gangster.

I took a job with an old family friend who was having a problem collecting money from builders who owed him a ton of money. He was a big-time cabinetmaker and employed a lot of people. Some builders were stiffing him on the cabinets they ordered and delivered. He could be in trouble soon if he did not collect the money so he asked me to help him. I had a reputation for doing this kind of work, probably because of the company I kept. When I showed up on the job site, the builders would whip out their checkbooks and start writing checks. Word travelled that Lafata's hitman was on the way so the check was ready before I arrived. I collected almost all the outstanding debt within three months and, in essence, worked my way out of a good job. I never raised my voice or had to lean on anyone. Sometimes the look is more powerful than any deed. It worked for me. What happened next surprised me. The owner of the company asked me if I would be interested in staying to help evaluations of the workforce, make recommendations, and implement necessary changes. I felt that with some small adjustments, the company's overall productivity could be improved and waste could be minimized to reflect a substantial change to the bottom line. I loved the owner but working with the multiple family members proved to be exceedingly difficult.

After one particularly stressful day, Jinny asked me why I could not do the same thing for her company. I said, "Why not!" Then I gave my notice the next day. Little did I know, this choice would be significant in shaping the rest of our lives. Jinny and I began spending a lot of time together. We were good for each other. To put it in Jinny's words that she borrowed from the movie *Rocky*, "You got gaps, and I got gaps. Together we kind a fill each other's gaps. We fit together." I think that was her attempt to be a wise guy.

Again, as was my habit, I excluded God from everything. I had this; I was back in control of my life. Instead of saying, "Jesus, take the wheel," I told Him to get in the back seat while I do my own driving. Jinny and I had moved in together and we were having a great time planned a future that did not include Him. Still I needed Him to stay in the background in case I had to bounce something off Him or blame Him once in a while. In one of our late-night talks, I asked Jinny to dream. I told her to dream big. What she wanted if she could have anything. She said she always wanted to own a day spa where an average person could enjoy beauty services, not just the rich people. She also was emphatic that she wanted a place where the stylists and other employees could retire from if they chose to. A place that could afford benefits and would not be so transient like other hair salons. She asked me what my dream was, I told her I could sell anything I honestly believed in. As long as it involved people, I was good with anything. A hair salon was a challenge, but I could make it work. We began laying out a plan.

12

God Gives Me a Workmate

This woman was no joke. We both dove into this project, but Jinny was amazing. She would work all day long doing hair and most of the night doing research. I was a talker. I could explain our vision to anyone and get people to buy into our plan, but this girl could move mountains. Our styles were completely different and quite honestly would clash…a lot. I watched her be in perpetual motion, moving things back and forth and making sure everything had to be in the exact place while I was sitting in a chair, drinking a cup of coffee, smoking a cigarette, and putting this picture into my head to go move an item just once. I would get exhausted watching her move widgets. When I called her out on it, that usually resulted in us getting into fights. Then one day, I made a comment based on my observation of her that I stand by to this day, however she took it as an insult. I held many jobs up to this time in my life—from a factory worker, Pepsi delivery driver, restaurant owner, auto-reconditioning shop owner—but never in my life had I met anyone, men or women, who could outwork Jinny. She is a pit bull. She was mad as hell that I said this to one of our customers. I could not win.

My gift was speaking. I had no problem making friends. I traveled from hair salon to hair salon and hit every cosmetology school in the Metro Detroit area, building relationships with administrators, owners, and students alike. They would invite me to do speaking engagements on business building. In return, the schools would send us the cream of the crop of students after they would graduate. I traveled all over the country attending hair shows and got on a first name basis with all the top product manufactures. I booked television appearances for our salon staff on shows that did extreme makeovers and arranged for all our local community support projects to drive awareness for our business. While in the development stage, I went around and did a survey of hairstylists. I wanted to know two things, what was the favorite thing they wanted to do with their careers and what part of the business did they hate the most. The consensus was they wanted to become colorists. The thing they universally hated doing the most was children's haircuts. They said they would go so far as to refuse to cut children's hair and send them to other salons.

I called our equipment designer and asked them if they carried any products like animated chairs or other furniture for children. They said they had a brochure with a couple of items in it so I asked them to bring the blueprint design of our new salon with them. I scrapped the original design against the arguments of the "professional" designers. I told them I wanted a huge children's salon built inside of our salon right by our front window. At my urging, our landlord decided to build an extension to the strip center we were located in. I was involved right from the planning stages and signed a lease agreement that would give us the end location on the busiest intersection in our county. This allowed for double signage on the outside of the building. After the construction began, the landlord kept coming back to me, telling me this company or that company wanted the corner. I just waived the legal document to him and told him to take a walk. One day, he showed up with a signed offer from Dairy Queen. I gave him the corner. It would turn out to be a brilliant move for many years to come. I got to where I could estimate our children's hair sales by how much ice cream was smeared on our windows from the night before. I also recruited a high-end children's clothing resale shop to move into the other side of us. If you had kids and you lived in our community, you were coming to our corner.

Did I tell you that Jinny was the hardest working person I ever met? She singlehandedly decorated this whole new salon. After a full days' work as a hairstylist, she painted the children's salon, which we named Kids Kuts, in all primary colors. We bought Barbie Jeeps and four-wheelers that the kids could sit in and a big-screen television to watch cartoons on. We also had children's music playing in the background. We even had a big green frog that kids could sit on while they had a haircut. The method to my madness was that if hairstylists hated cutting children's hair, they would be sending all the kids over to us. I would train up all our new stylists right out of cosmetology school to grow their clientele by cutting children's hair while talking to the parents and offering to do their entire family. We could be the hair salon for the entire family. Their job was to communicate with the parents while making the most precious things the parents possessed, their children, both happy and beautiful. Our break-even point was fifty haircuts per week. We did 150 the very first week and were up to 500 per week by Christmas on our first year.

However, it was not without its challenges. The day before our grand opening, most of our staff quit. They wanted no part of my ideas and resented me being involved in the business at all. I was not a hairdresser. It would prove to be the biggest mistake of their careers. That night, and many soon after, it hurt like hell. I was blaming God all over again. Why did He continue to curse me? I was angry. Just thinking of that day now, I can recall the sickening feeling in the pit of my stomach, but it strengthened our resolve. Jinny said, "We will make it through this. I will work behind the chair with five or six girls. You work behind the counter and get busy with the cosmetology schools." Many of the hairdressers who had left us came to ask for their positions back after we became the largest salon in Troy, Michigan.

Jinny had two daughters from her first marriage who did not approve of our relationship. Their disapproval was not on a moral ground, they just had their issues. They saw me moving in on their territory. No matter how hard I tried, they were having none of it. Add to this mistrust, they just saw Jinny as someone who did not know what she was doing. They could not understand what she saw in me. We were in this together now. It was sink or swim, and neither one of us had life jackets. Her daughters both worked for us and eventually most of the grandchildren. Jinny and I had butted heads on the issues of her daughters and their work style…or lack thereof.

Still there are benefits and curses in having family work for you. We experienced them both.

Jinny's grandson spent the night with us. In the morning, he asked me if I was going to be his grandpa. That was not in the plan, but it got both of us thinking that it was not right for us sleeping together in front of the grandchildren. Jinny's oldest granddaughter was the next one to start pushing for us to get married because she wanted to plan the wedding. She was about six at the time.

I was always joking with Jinny about her never ironing any of our clothes. I knew it would irk her so I laid it on pretty thick. I would tell her how my mother would iron everything, including my socks and underwear. If we were to get married, she would have to look after me in the manner I had grown accustom to. She would just roll her eyes and tell me to go live with my mother. I told her the biggest mistake I ever made in my life was leaving my mother's house. I had it made, which was the truth.

I decided to make an honest woman out of her so I bought an engagement ring. I also bought a small compact ironing board and taped the ring box to the board. I proposed to her by asking her if she would iron my clothes for the rest of our lives. Through her tears, she said yes. She lied. She never used the ironing board and never owned an iron, for all I knew. What I got out of this was the knowledge that I was the only man I knew who was so bold to propose in such a manner and live to talk about it. The other thing I got out of it was something that would take a few more years for me to find out. God had given me a second angel.

Jinny and Frank's Wedding Photo

13

A Light at the End of the Tunnel

We let Jinny's six-year-old granddaughter be our wedding planner. She went shopping with her grandma and bought all the decorations. She wanted to decorate my mother's basement where we would hold our reception. We just had immediate family and a few good friends as guests. The wedding chapel used to be a cigar shop that a couple of entrepreneurs converted into a chapel like the ones they have in Las Vegas. All that was missing was a drive-through window. We were not too serious about this program.

We met with the pastor who turned out to be a woman. She asked us several questions about the wedding day: how many people will be attending, how many bridesmaids and groomsmen, and would we prefer her or her husband to perform the service. Jinny and I looked at each other, determined that the men who performed her previous three marriages and the guys that did my previous two didn't seem to have the magic to make them last so we thought we would try our luck with the woman. She then told us to have our wedding party come to the chapel the day before the wedding for rehearsal. To practice walking down the aisle. I told her, "Ma'am, between all our previous marriages, we have worn out carpets walking up these aisles." We had a good laugh.

The wedding went off with only one glitch. I oversaw buying the wedding cake, so I ordered a bunch of cheesecakes that my sister decorated. The problem with this is the grandchildren hated cheesecake so I was on the bad person list. How could I make such a huge error? The other mistake was God was not invited to the wedding.

We were back to work on Monday. Any honeymoon would have to wait. We were focused on growing the business and making lots of money. We had gone so long without money that we were loving having some. We hired any kind of people as long as they could make us money. We were open seven days a week. If the employees refused to work Sunday or before any major holidays, they were let go. I found people who were driven to succeed. Gay, straight, divorcees, kids just out of school, alcoholics—it did not matter. If they could produce, they could work for us. Our clientele included kids, families, bachelors, senior citizens, and cross-dressers. We even had a hair extension service that targeted strippers.

With my background in the restaurant business, I had a rather large kitchen and break room for the employees. I would cook several times a week because we were so busy, the employees did not have time to go and eat. Whatever they wanted; I would make pizza, hamburgers, roast beef, turkey, chicken parmesan, spaghetti and meatballs, salads, fruit plates, soups and chili for them. The smells of my cooking would waft into the salon. Customers came back in just to see what I was cooking. I would feed them too. It was hilarious. The usually slowest time for booking appointments in the day was noontime, but now the clients would book their appointments between eleven and one o'clock just so they could have lunch their in their appointment. I never charged the clients or staff for food. It was my joy to do this for them, and it was good for business. I would be at the supermarket buying my groceries, and women would stop me to ask what I was cooking for lunch and when I was making one of their favorites, so they could book their appointments.

The health department got wind of what I was doing. A guy stopped in and said I had to stop cooking because I did not have a license to cook food. I told him that I was cooking my lunch. It was my business with whom I wanted to share my lunch. I told him I never charged anyone for sharing my lunch with them. He did not know what to do with me. I honestly did not know if he was more scared of me or all those hungry women who were staring daggers at him. Unfortunataely, most good things must come to an end, what was intended for good ended up getting destroyed by the attitudes of a few. The staff were resentful that the clients could invade "their" break room and eat "their" food. They had no problem telling other staff member's clientele off for trespassing on their turf. That started a war. The complaining was nonstop, "You know I don't eat this or that. You're just doing it on purpose." They sucked the joy right out of making something nice for everybody. I eventually stopped cooking.

My buddies would stop by and visit occasionally. We were so busy most of the time, I did not have time to visit with them. They would just sit in the waiting room chairs until I got freed up. Then they would come into my office. "How do you do it?" they would ask. "These women are so beautiful and hot. How do you not get into so much trouble?" Now don't get me wrong, we had many wonderful young women and some not so young who worked for us throughout the years, but for the most part, my response to my buddies was very truthful. I would tell them that beauty is only skin deep, but ugly goes right through to the bone. When you spent as much time with some of these "beauties," you would know exactly what I mean.

I had worked in many different venues over the years. I had worked with some of the toughest, grouchiest, and meanest men you would ever meet. However, none of them could be as mean-spirited, hateful, deceitful, foul-mouthed, and vengeful as some of these women could be. When guys in my day got in a beef with each other, they followed a pretty standard set of unspoken rules. First was the trash talk. If that went too far or, God forbid, someone was stupid enough to mention the other guy's mother, you knew battle was coming with the "stare." Blows would start flying in most cases, followed by being separated by close friends or other guys in the area. More trash talk and a volley of cursing. But that was it. It was pretty much put to rest, sometimes within minutes. It would culminate in a respectful handshake with a newfound respect that the other guy stood his ground. Allies were formed this way, which could grow into lasting friendships. Does it go this way all the time? Heck no! That is why prisons are full of mostly men who never learned the *rules* of conflict resolution. Some could not handle their own battles and hired a "hit." Most guys are doing hefty prison sentences just because they could not control their tempers or they felt disrespected.

Women, on the other hand, if you piss them off for anything, they make you their enemy for life. You read about how women are the gentler or softer sex, the more loving sex. That is bull! They will rip each other's hearts out in a nanosecond. They do not make friends easily. They will introduce other women as their best friend only to leave them on a bar stool, just for the chance to hook up with a guy who gave them a second look. I've seen women sitting together, holding each other as one pours her heart out to the other one only to come back an hour later to see the best friend trash-talking the women who just confided in them to anyone who will listen. There is no code of conduct. These wars could be anything from stealing another women's boyfriend and or husband to simply being indifferent to a new hairstyle. "Who does that B think she is, dissing me that way? She thinks she is better than me? I will show her!" Next thing you know, cliques are forming. War meetings are taking place. Before you know it, the whole business is going to hell in a handbasket.

I spent more time counseling my staff than anything. I learned that no matter how high my desk was piled up with work or how many phone calls I had on hold, if one of the girls stuck their heads in my office, the conversation would generally go something like this, "Frank, are you busy?" I would reply, "Oh no, honey. Come on in." I would turn my back to them in my swivel chair, locate a box of Kleenex that I would keep stock piled up in the corner, utter a little prayer to a God I barely knew for guidance then I would turn around and the tears would flow as they would talk about anything and everything. And I mean anything. Let me say no to them or that I was busy, they were sure to leave for greener pastures. They would not work for someone so insensitive, they would tell me at their exit interview. "You are mad at me because I did not have time to listen about your sick cat?" It did not matter. I learned if it was important enough for them to come to talk to me about it, everything better stop. As if this was not bad enough, trying to figure out all the mood swings and the multiple personalities of these women, God forbid, I would have one of the gay guys come to my office to "talk." The drama that would ensue would be unbelievable. When they left my office crying, a line would form of girls wanting to know everything that transpired. I wanted to scream.

I was a slow learner, I must admit. I had trouble trying to figure out what made these folks tick at first. But I did learn after rebuilding my business several times. I discovered that as much as I wanted to be friends with my employees, it was better for everyone if they could have one common enemy they could rally against instead of fighting each other. They decided that enemy was me. In time, this would ease up. When I would learn of a new technique for the office visits that never stopped, I will share this with you later.

My wife was one of them. She was out among the floor staff all day long. She would catch a comment here and there and surmise that I was stirring the pot again. She never took the time to listen to anyone for exceptionally long because she was just too busy. She would have two or three chairs of clients going at a time. Wrapping a perm in one, placing color on another, and giving a haircut all at the same time. Did I tell you she was the hardest working person I ever met? She came across to our staff as being totally insensitive to them. They knew not to mess with Jinny when she was on a roll, and she was always on a roll. Jinny would walk by my office just long enough to throw a match on a tinderbox situation then she was off to take care of customers, leaving me to spend the next hour or two putting out the fire. I was exhausted.

Although we only lived two miles from the salon at this time, we never rode together to work. Sometimes we would follow each other to and from work, but we always took separate cars. Maybe we just wanted to have those few moments of alone time or maybe just to take the time to calm down before we needed to interact. We spent twelve hours in the same building, and many times we had never even exchanged a word. More likely, we wished we had not exchanged a word. We would grab some takeout for dinner and just collapse at home. When she did talk, she would say something like, "I did $1,000 in business today." I would explode, "That's great. I put out thousands of dollars in fires today. People quitting, hiring new people, and setting up training for all the brand-new stylists."

The thing I could never understand was she had a hands-on personality. She was perpetual motion. If she was not moving, she was not
working, to her mind. I tried to get her to understand that her true
value in our business was her knowledge that she stored in her head.
Instead of doing all this physical work, if she could just spend some
time with our thirty-five employees and teach them the absolute
minimum skills to improve their productivity just ten percent, she
would have tripled her production. "What about twenty percent?"
She just could not get what I was saying, and this never changed.
Most of her clients were elderly. She was doing roller sets on them at
prices they were paying when she started doing them forty years ago.
In the meantime, the newer clients that were coming into our salon
were offended if they "only" paid a hundred bucks for their services
because their girlfriends in Birmingham and Bloomfield were paying
several times that much. Jinny was so loyal to her old clients that
it cost us a small fortune. But this is what made Jinny who she is.
Sometimes that is more valuable than money. I would learn that later.
For the time being, we would go to bed mad at each other again.

All this stress was getting to us. We kept buying stuff, trying to
fill the void we were feeling with things. Cars, gifts for family mem-
bers, and mostly homes. We bought a timeshare in Florida and went
down there for a one-week vacation with a couple of my cousins.
During that time, it rained like I have never seen before. Hurricane
Josephine was a direct hit. Everything was flooded. The girls wanted
to go look at some condominiums on this golf course community.
We were walked into the very first model and my cousin Tony said
I want it. I want this very unit with everything just the way it sits.
He was ready to write a check right there on the spot. I thought he
was nuts. The place was beautiful and all, but he did not even make
an offer to negotiate the price or anything. I never paid asking price
for anything in my life. Hell, half the fun was in the haggling. I had
always looked up to Tony growing up, but this was a game changer.
He was crazy. We went back to our room. Jinny started doing the
math and said it made sense as an investment. We could rent it out
for three months a year and use it the rest of the year. It will pay for
itself. We needed someplace to get away from the stress. She was

really excited about it. I could never say no to anything she wanted. To this day, this remains true. She worked so hard for everything she ever got out of life. Did I tell you she was the hardest working person I ever knew? The next day, we signed the papers, and they began building our unit.

Within a year, we were buying another home in the same golf community. Jinny and my sister Maryjo went for a walk in the complex. Maryjo and her husband Harold, my brother-in-law (more like my brother), had been going through some tough times with one of their daughters. It had taken its toll on them. That night, Jinny said we should go in with them and buy another brand-new home. It was big and beautiful, and it would do wonders for them. What the heck, another mortgage? That would make it our third. Within another year and a half, mortgages number 4 and 5 would happen. What was wrong with these lending institutions? Were they crazy lending someone like me all this money? We seldom even use these vacation homes because every time we went away, it would cost us way more than the price of the vacation. Our staff also helped themselves to unauthorized pay raises, family included. It was heartbreaking, literally.

14

My God, What Is Happening?

I was at home laying on the couch with my foot elevated, my foot was inflamed with one of the worse gout attacks I had in years. It was a condition I suffered with for my entire adult life. I did not know it then, but heart disease was also beginning to take its toll on me. The phone rang. It was Jinny on the other end. "You have a visitor at the salon." *What was wrong with her, couldn't she just leave me alone for one day to rest and get this thing under control?* I asked miserably, "Who is it?" She replied, "It's your daughter Karen. She wants to see you."

I had not seen Karen since her mother divorced me. Stepparents do not have parental visitation rights in our court system. Something that really needs to get fixed. I could not have loved those kids anymore if I had been their biological father. To be more accurate, she had not seen me for years. I kept track of her through friends of hers who came to the salon. I would go to several of her volleyball, basketball, and soccer games, sitting way up in the far corner of the bleachers to go unnoticed. I would drive by their house many times, hoping to just get a glimpse of them. Now she wanted to see me. She asked me to meet her down the street at the local Denny's. I left the house, not even trying to put a shoe on that gouty foot. I arrived at the restaurant in about twenty minutes on what would have been a normal forty-minute trip.

I saw her sitting in a booth facing me. My heart leapt with joy, but something inside me told me not to hug her as much as I wanted to. As I sat down, she began unloading on me for everything that went wrong in her life since I left. She blamed me for everything.

Apparently, her mother vented on them about what she thought was the cause of the split. I swore never to say a negative thing to the kids about their mother. I figured there was no point. I could try to explain to them, but in the end, I would still lose them for good anyway. I could never understand how anybody could raise themselves up in another person's eyes by putting someone else down, regardless of how righteous they felt. This went on for close to an hour. Then she got up and left. It hurt so badly, but just being in her presence was wonderful. She called back in a couple of days and wanted to meet at the same place again. She still had a few other things to get off her chest. I did not say a word in my own defense. I just wanted her to know that I still loved her and would always love her no matter what she thought of me. I never liked it when people say something like "I did the best I could under the circumstances because I never knew what my best was." I would just have to own this if I could have her in my life again. Even if her truth was not the truth. She would have to learn this lesson later in her life when she had her own children.

Things were getting better. She was always one of the funniest people I ever knew. After all, she was mine, so we laughed a lot. The third time she called, she asked if Jinny and I would like to join her at a new church next Sunday. It was really cool, she said. They were meeting in the Troy High School auditorium. Church in a school was a new one to me. I must be completely honest here, I could not have cared less if it were a church, a mosque, a synagogue, a Hare Krishna chanting circle, or a WWF wrestling match. If she was going there, so was I. I cried through the whole service. I know now that God was crying, too, and was saying, the same thing. "My son is back in My house."

The church was called Kensington Community Church. They were moving into a large new building a few miles from the school. We attended these services every Sunday. I met some really cool people. I was still a football junkie, a Detroit Lions fan. That tells you that I was used to disappointments in my life. The associate pastor was the Detroit Lions' team chaplain. A few of the Lions attended church there. One day, Luther Ellis, who was one of the only All-Pro defensive tackles in Lions' history, asked me if I would like to attend a

Bible study with him. Luther and I had become friends. He brought his entire family to our salon for haircuts. He loved kids so much that as fast as him and his wife were having them, he was adopting even more. I think he ended up with like a dozen kids, and he would bring them in for haircuts in vans. The only thing that this guy loved more than his wife and children was his Lord. He was amazing.

One day, the church announced that they were going to have this event called Marriage Encounter. The theme was "Marriage on the Rock," which seemed an appropriate description of my marriage. It was close to crashing on the rocks. Jinny asked me to go. It was for an entire weekend, but not just any weekend. It was during Super Bowl Sunday, the holiest of hollies for football junkies. One thing we never had to worry about that weekend though was the Detroit Lions never played in the Super Bowl since their inception. I went kicking and screaming. After all, I could not find it in me to say no to this woman even when I was pissed at her. This was going to be horrible. I had already made up my mind. True to form, Friday night was miserable. How did I let this happen? Saturday started out about the same, but then things started to take a turn. There were a couple hundred people there who were called into a big meeting room where Pastor Dave Wilson was speaking on a raised platform. He was walking back and forth on the platform and talking about marriage, but I was not listening to him at all. I was hearing an inner voice that was so hard to explain. It was talking to me. Only me. It was saying, *Do you see that cross? Do you know that I would have gone up on that cross and endured all that pain if it were just for you? If nobody else in the world were involved, I would have taken that cross for you, Frank.*

Tears started streaming down my face. Pastor Dave kept talking and pacing, but now he seemed to look right at me, sitting only three rows back. My heart started talking back to this voice. *I could understand, Lord, how You could forgive all these other people for all the sins they committed, but how could You ever forgive me for all the times I turned my back on You,* I asked silently. I was openly sobbing now, so lost. Then He said to me, *You were lost, my son. Now you are found. Come, follow Me.* I accepted His invitation and turned my life and my heart over to Him right then and there. Dave stared at this gorilla in the third row who was crying like a baby. I stood up and asked him to stop. I told him in front of all these strange people I did not know what just happened, that Jesus just asked me to surrender my life to Him, which I did. The room erupted as if the Lions just scored the winning touchdown in the Super Bowl. It was bigger than that to me.

We broke for lunch. Everyone seemed to be seeking me out to either congratulate me, welcome me into the kingdom of believers, or to tell me their stories of when and how they were called to the Lord. It was awesome! We resumed by meeting in rooms separated by men and women. We sat around tables of eight men and were led in prayer by one of the elders. He asked us to go around the table and say one thing that we wanted everyone to pray about. When it was my turn, I mentioned my daughter Karen. She had gone off and joined Americore and was sent to live in a little shack in some backwoods rural area of Montana to work with kids in that community. I was terrified that she would run into a bear or something on her mountain hikes with the kids (*Poor bear*, I thought). More than that, I was afraid she would meet some mountain man and never come back to Michigan. I just got her back into my life and off she goes to fix the world. I wanted her to meet a good Christian man and settle down *in Michigan* with me and give me some grandchildren to spoil. All the guys got a chuckle out of my self-centeredness, even with my prayer. The young man next to me recently got married. He prayed for his younger brother, asking God for a good woman for him. We joked about hooking up my daughter with his brother. I never met this boy before, but I sure liked him. If his brother was anything like him, he would sure fit the bill for my Karen.

When we left that Sunday, I was on an emotional high like I never have been in my life. I wanted to shout and sing His praises. I wanted to take on the world for Christ. I wanted to rush off into battle against the forces of evil for my Lord and Savior, Jesus Christ. I got back to the Bible study with Luther. He was so happy for me but issued a warning, "Slow down, young puppy (I was a good twenty years his senior). You're still eating spiritual puppy chow. You need to learn about the armor of God then eat grown-up spiritual food, the Word of God." It would take a while.

Within a couple of weeks, I suffered another heart attack. I was in and out of the hospital several times and had stents put in only to have them clog up time and time again, seven in total. The doctors said I needed to have another open-heart surgery. I went to see the surgeon who did my first open-heart surgery ten years ago. He looked at my tests and said no way and declined. He was convinced that if he had to open me up again, there was a good chance of cutting into the mammary gland he used to bypass the aneurism he repaired before. He said I could bleed out on the table. It was better for me to live out what time I had left.

I went home feeling dejected, but I could not give up. I came close, but I had never given up on anything in my life. I had God on my side. I was not going anywhere until He was done with me. I started researching the top heart specialists in the country and found one right in my own backyard. I made an appointment and went to see him. He examined my records and said he was willing to give it a try, but he was not making any promises. It was going to be very risky. It would be best to have my affairs in order just in case. It was not exactly what I wanted to hear, but the surgery date was set. God listens to the prayers of a loving mother. He had His hands full with my mother, sisters, aunts, and nieces. They were not about to let go of me. They were bombarding the throne room of God with prayers. Jinny was awesome. She took care of the business all by herself and keep everyone sane in the family as well. She even bought an airline ticket for Karen so she could be with me for the surgery. It was just what I needed. I was surrounded by all my family, I was right with my Lord, and my buddies were there just in case. I was ready for any outcome.

When the surgery was over, the surgeon asked Jinny and my family if they knew how wide two millimeters was. He stood a piece of paper on its edge, indicating how thick it really was. When they used the saw to cut into my chest cavity, one doctor asked another, "Is that what I think it is?" The blade of the saw was resting on the mammary gland bypass. He commented that someone up there was looking after me. It could have been game over.

Karen had a few days before she had to head back to Montana. She stayed with me and visited friends at Kensington Church where she met a young man named Matt. In time, he became my son-in-law. A real gift from God. Before they got married, Karen set up a luncheon where Jinny and I and Karen's mother would meet Matt's family. I immediately recognized Matt's older brother. He was the same guy I had held hands with and prayed with on the day I gave my life to Jesus. How great is this God we serve?

Big Papa, Grandma Jin, and the Grandkids

15

The Forty Days of Purpose

I often wondered how the Israelites and early Christians who walked with Jesus and witnessed such awesome miracles could still be so stubborn and hard-hearted. They had to be a special kind of stupid to see people raised from the dead, the parting of the Red Sea, sick people healed, and still have doubts, rebellion, and disbelief. What was wrong with those people? How did God tolerate such foolishness? How could He not just give up on those fools? Because God is faithful, that is why.

I become bitter. Karen went back to Montana. My family and friends also went back to their normal lives on the other side of town, far enough that they could not just drop by and visit. Jinny, saddled with a double load of running the business and doing her work as well as mine, was never home except to clean up around the house and go to sleep, only to arise and head back out to work. I was alone in a huge house, barely able to take care of myself. It was decided that I would go down to our house in Fort Myers, Florida, to recover. Jinny was never home so I might as well be someplace warm. As husband number four, I was sure that I was going to be replaced by husband number five soon. Before I left, I told Jinny that I wanted to move back across town to be closer to my people since I did not want to die alone.

My cousin Pat, who worked for us, came to work one day and told Jinny that she saw this small ranch-style house right around the block from her as she took a walk the night before. It was only a mile away from both of my sisters and a couple of blocks from where I grew up. The next night, we drove over there. It was only thirty-five minutes away so it would not be too bad for Jinny to drive to work from there. We spent only ten minutes there when Jinny looked at me and said, "I can do this." We bought the place right on the spot. Small problem, we had not sold the house we were living in and we had two other houses in Florida. Add a bridge loan so we could close on this one, we now had five mortgages. I did not care. *She and her new husband could figure it out*, I thought bitterly.

Jinny told me to just go to Florida. She would have everything worked out when I came back in a couple of months. I told her, "Just tell me where my pillow is, and I will go right there." I was lucky she did not put that pillow over my head or next to the curb. I was so frustrated and depressed. When I came back from Florida two and a half months later, our house had still not sold, and the house we put the offer on across town had not closed yet. I was back in that huge house all alone, not doing any better physically or mentally. Jinny was trying everything to lift my spirits, if not just to get me off her back. One day, she came home and told me that one of our receptionists' daughter bought a golden retriever puppy and realized after one week she could not take care of it. She wanted to know if we would take it. Everyone at the salon thought this was exactly what I needed to keep me company. The young girl brought the ten-week-old puppy over to the house the next night. Jinny and I both fell instantly in love with her. I named her Sancho, which means "trusted friend and companion." Jinny said the name is masculine for a female dog. I argued, "If this dog is going to be living with us it better get used to being confused." Jinny never had dogs before so she was in for a surprise with how much care they needed. I laid down the law, there will be no dogs on the furniture and under no circumstances will the dog be allowed in our bed.

By late fall, my cousins insisted that I go with them on our annual deer-hunting trip up north in the Michigan woods even if I could only handle a weekend. I agreed to go. They picked me up early Thursday morning and brought me home late Sunday night. Jinny was already in bed so I quietly made my way to the bedroom, sat on the edge of the bed, and began undressing. Sancho heard me and came running. She leaped up on the bed, curled up, and put her head on my pillow. Jinny, now awake, said, "By the way, not only does Sancho not think too much about your rules, she has taken a liking to your pillow. Her favorite spot is your chair in the living room." From that day on, the new boss of the house was this adorable golden bundle of joy. I credit that wonderful dog with saving my life and my marriage.

Sancho on the Couch

The house across town was ready. We closed and just left the house in Troy vacant. It remained vacant for almost a year before we sold it for the same price we were offered for it one week after we listed it, which we turned down initially. It cost us a small fortune. More dumb choices. I let my stubbornness keep me from doing what

God intended…again. He provided a buyer, but I closed the door in His face. When would I learn to listen?

The move was complete, but Jinny felt that it was just too far away from Kensington Church so she started looking for a new church closer to home. One Sunday, she went to a Pentecostal church a few miles away. She felt it was just too weird for her. She met a wonderful black woman who invited her to attend church with her the following week. Jinny came home the next week and told me that she just went to church in a really shady part of Detroit known as a Red Light district. The church services were held in a closed down triple X-rated movie theater. I went crazy. "What the heck is the matter with you? Where is your common sense? Are you in that big of a hurry to meet Jesus? You are going to get yourself killed!" I barked. "What possessed you to go there?" She said she was looking for another Pentecostal church. I asked her, "Do you even know what a Pentecostal church is?" She said, "I don't care what it is. Joyce Myers is Pentecostal, and that works for me."

I smacked my hand on my forehead. This woman was going to kill me or get herself killed, I felt sure of it. Things were getting crazier by the day. My frustration was causing argument after argument. Family strife and business problems, coupled with a mired of bad decisions, were tearing us apart. She would never answer the phone when I called, which added to my mistrust of her.

The following Sunday, we went to my mother's house for dinner. It was not a good day. I was ready to file for divorce and end this nightmare. We left my mothers and headed home. We were driving down a street called Ten Mile Road when we passed by an Assembly of God church that had a marque in front, advertising that they were starting a series that night on the book by Rick Warren called *The Purpose Driven Life*. I did an abrupt U-turn at the next intersection and drove back to the church parking lot. We both heard of this book. I looked at Jinny and said in all seriousness, "This is all I have left in me, forty days. I'm willing to go to this, but if this does not work, I'm out of here. You can go live in the other house, and we will get divorced."

We went to the church that night at six o'clock. We were greeted by a genuinely nice lady who escorted us to our seats. The pastor came out on a stage. He instantly reminded me of the actor Jim Carry. My first impression was that he was a real fruitcake. He was yelling and screaming, doing karate kicks, and then going totally silent in reverent prayer. I would learn to like the guy over time. It even turned into a kind of love that I ruined by putting him up on a pedestal. No man belongs on a pedestal. We are all humans. We all have faults.

Every morning for the next forty days, Jinny and I were praying together, reading a chapter a day out of the book, and answering the questions in the study guide. It was wonderful. All I wanted was for her to spend time with me. The church was great. We were meeting all kinds of new people. On the morning of day 41, I woke up to find Jinny gone. She had left me. After all, I set the terms. Forty days was the deal. I blew up her phone, trying to reach her. No response. I was devastated. All day long, my calls went unanswered. That evening, the garage door opened. Sancho jumped off my lap and ran to the door to greet her mommy. Jinny came in the house with the biggest smile on her face, praising God. She was on a high like I had not ever seen her.

I took her into my arms and thanked God she came home. She asked why I seemed so shocked to see her. I said, "I thought you left me for another guy. Why didn't you answer your phone?" She said, "Oh, I forgot to charge it, and it went dead." It was so typical of Jinny. I smacked my head again.

The truth was, I did lose Jinny to another man that day. His name was Jesus. I would have to share her with Him for the rest of our lives and for all of eternity. I also know who is first in her life, and it sure is not me.

16

A Change of Hearts

We were both on fire for the Lord. We turned our entire lives over to Him. We woke up every morning and gave Him praise for a new day. We confessed all transgressions to Him and asked Him to forgive us. We thanked Him for even the smallest of things, trying not to forget any blessings He had given us. Finally, we asked Him for everything that we thought we might need to complete our day, from additional wisdom, guidance, or boldness to anything that came into our minds. We were not going through it alone again. He was at the center of everything in our lives. He would be consulted in all decisions from that day forward. I came across a bumper sticker that said, "If God is your copilot, then you are in the wrong seat. I was lucky to even have Him in the back seat of my car in the past. No more. We pledged to go where He led us, loving every minute of the ride. We were now truly born again. Soon we would also experience the baptism of the Holy Spirit. Jinny went first. My baptism would come later. I was happy for her. I felt like I was lacking something until the day I became spirit-filled. There was no stopping us now.

Jinny became involved in the women's ministries. She was so intimidated when she was asked to join the women's Bible study. After the first one, she came home nervous from being there with all those churchwomen. She spent most of the night walking around the house praying in the spirit. In the morning, she was perfectly calm. I asked her what changed. She said she just turned her fear over to the Lord. He instructed her to go to the next Bible study and "do it afraid." He would be with her through it all. Within a year, she was teaching Bible study to new believers.

I was still playing it safe. I joined too many churches in the past only to be disappointed. The pastor's wife gave me a tour and a run-down of all their services. I told her I would be spending every Sunday morning at the Sunrise Service on the first hole of the golf course as my buddies and I have done for decades. She kind of laughed at me and told me that if I continued to walk along the river's edge with Jesus, eventually I would fall in and as far as my buddies. She told me to tell them that I was practicing for the Master's Tournament. We continued our walk through the building and found the social hall that had a beautiful stainless steel kitchen. The pastor's wife said it was seldom used at all. I informed her that was about to change. I found my ministry. I began cooking meals for the whole church for fundraisers, weekly outreaches to the community, and even a wedding reception or two. I put together a team of volunteers who knew what they were doing around a kitchen and a few that were clueless (one guy, in particular).

Jinny and I arrived early for our first Wednesday night service. We were sitting alone at a large circular table for eight. In walked this guy who was at least four hundred pounds. He had a scowl on his face and a demeanor about him that could turn a piece of wood to ashes with just a glance. Jinny told me to ask him to sit with us. I did, but he just continued to walk by like we were not even there. The following week, the same thing. Jinny gives me "the look." In the past, this is the kind of scenario that would have prompted me to get up and get in the guy's face for disrespecting my wife. I had an edge in my tone as I invited him to have a seat with us. He grunted something and sat down. I jokingly blamed my wife for this day for the next twenty years.

To protect his anonymity (he hates being recognized and God forbid if someone takes his picture), we will call him John for our purposes. The Holy Spirit made this divine appointment for both of us. I look at John as my antithesis. I was loud, talkative, thoughtful, and a people person. John was the opposite. We came from the same streets and business world, but our responses were totally different. John got knocked down. He was in the bar business lost it and became a drunk. His wife left him, which started his spiral down. One similarity is that we both have a good sense of humor and the ability to laugh at ourselves. We better have, the way Jesus keeps messing with us. I can actually envision our Lord having a big belly laugh looking at the situations we get ourselves into. John completely owned up to his plight and thankfully restored his relationship with his two grown children and he absolutely adores his grandchildren. They, along with his ex-wife and her husband, include John in their holidays and family functions. Most of the time, he came back from these visits with his spirit lifted. When I ask him how it went, he always says great. I think my ex is just about ready to apologize for leaving me." We would laugh. I had the opportunity to meet her once at the wedding of their son. When someone pointed her out to me from across the room, I walked over to her and, without even an introduction, I asked her what I ever did to her that she would saddle me with John. The kids must have told her about me so when she realized who I was, she started laughing and said, "Better you than me. I did my time." She seemed like a special lady.

John became a staple in my family. Everyone loved him. He has a tremendous memory, too good at times, and is a walking, talking appointment book. If I had a doctor's appointment, a business meeting, or a fishing trip, he wanted to know when, who was going to be there, what time I was leaving, and when I was coming back. It drives me crazy because if I asked him about anything in his life, he would answer, "It's none of your business." In a way, he has become an external hard drive of my memory and more so, my spiritual compass.

When it comes to the kitchen, he is about as useful as a second thumb. The guy cannot peel a potato, much less the hundreds of pounds of potatoes we had to peel. It took him forever to peel just one, and the result looked more like a chicken nugget in size. One time when we were doing a large fundraiser for the choir at our church, I decided to cook an Italian feast that was going to blow everyone away. I enlisted the help of my family and the whole church's cooking team. We decided that the dessert table would have all the homemade cakes, pies, and huge hot fudge cream puffs with chocolate-dipped strawberries. John wanted to work on that, dipping huge strawberries into melted chocolate for hours. I put our friend Becky in charge of keeping him supplied with strawberries and melting the chocolate. When I came back several hours later to check on their progress, my jaw dropped to the floor. John was still sitting there, covered with chocolate. He looked like a giant chocolate statue. He had gotten more chocolate on him than on the berries. I looked at Becky, and she started to laugh so hard. She loved him so much she did not have the heart to tell him to stop. I guess the Lord was trying to teach me patience. I was obviously a slow learner. It was going to take some time.

Several years later, when God was ready to move Jinny and I several hundred miles away, John who was a constant at our home by now and had several meals with us a week was devastated. Before we left, I told him that I had put him in the purchase agreement with the new owners of the house. I hoped he liked Chinese because we had sold the house to a Chinese woman. He did not appreciate the attempt at humor to lighten his mood. God was not done with us. He was just giving us a break so I could focus on something bigger. John would go back into his shell and became a hermit again.

Things at the salon were still pretty horrible. We were still hiring young girls right out of beauty school. Their parents would bring some of them in to meet us because of all the wonderful things they heard about Jinny and me. Looking into these parents' eyes, I could see the trust they were placing in us. Now before I go any farther, let me try and explain something. We do not have a prejudiced bone in either of our bodies. Even before we found the Lord when our focus was making money, we were not judgmental. To tell you the truth, I was not proud of what was taking place in our business. Greedy, self-centered egotistical, petty, deceitful, and vindictive were only some of the adjectives I would use to describe some of our staff and many of our customers. It made me sick. I also felt like a hypocrite to be serving my Lord on a few days of the week and being responsible for this den of iniquity. The looks in those parents' eyes were haunting. What kind of example were we promoting to our own children and grandchildren? That night, we prayed to the Lord and asked him to help me take out the trash and turn our business into something we could be proud of and be used to serve Him.

The next day, we had a mandatory staff meeting where we announce that we were going to be making several changes. First of all, we would no longer be opened on Sunday. We wanted that day for them to spend with their family and go to church. Second of all, there would be no more perverse language. We had two gay guys and several married employees who were having affairs with other staff members who felt that it was fine to talk openly about their sexual exploits right in front of the new kids. This was over. We told them that we knew that God had a better plan for them and us. We warned them first but if it persisted, they would be terminated. Two days later, half of our staff quit and took over a million dollars' of annual business with them. Business that I had generated. It affected our family as well. My cousin who I had grown up with and loved, left with them and took copies of all our client lists. I would find out that she left for other reasons that would be revealed to me later. Apparently, there were a few termites left behind. I was on my knees again, calling out to God. "When I asked you to take out the trash, Lord. I did not mean all in one day. How would we survive? What have I done? What could I do now? Who was going to leave next?" My father's words came back to me. *Who are you going to serve?*

It was right before Christmas, the busiest time of the year for our industry. Our advertising representative from our local newspaper came in to see if I wanted to place an ad in their holiday edition. I thought for a second and then asked how much it would take to buy the entire back page of their newspaper. It was not cheap, since it was the holiday season, but I began writing my ad. The newspaper came out in the first week of December. All the holiday ads were in it so it was the paper everyone was looking for to see what was on sale. The back cover on the top of the page was the cross of Christ with my adoration for our Lord and Savior. I spoke of how mighty He was and that He could do all things. I confessed to all our customers in the community that I let them down for turning our business into something that we were no longer proud of. We promised to do better. I thanked all of our clients for enduring this dark time. I thanked

God for forgiving our trespasses and pledged our total reliance on Him. The first goal for our business would be to give all glory to Him. I asked God to guide us through these troubling waters and to bless all who entered our doors, both clients and employees alike. I lastly thanked Him for giving us His son Jesus Christ this Christmas season.

My intent on this ad was just to publicly give all glory to God. But do you know that you can never out give God? The phones rang off the hook. We had to add two more receptionists to answer all the calls and booking appointments. We got calls from people who were not even clients, thanking us for the ad. We got calls from past clients who left us before because of how they felt the direction our business was headed. Hairstylists were asking to work for us because they were sick of their current salons. I could now honestly look into the faces of the parents of the new kids coming in for the first time and tell them their daughter was in good hands with us and, more importantly, with Christ.

17

Be Careful What You Pray For

In the summer of 2001, things were going really well. The business was cranking, we were making good money paying off all our debts. We even sold a few properties. We were down to two mortgages so I was feeling kind of wealthy. We got really involved with the church, helping all kinds of people. I was cooking up a storm, and the church was growing. The board of the church decided to up their game and bring in a top headliner singer from the Gather Vocal Band, David Phelps and his whole entourage. They asked me if I would be in charge of the meals for everyone during the weekend stay. The management team sent an advance letter with their dietary requests. I ignored them. They were getting Italian food: chicken Parmesan with a side of pasta, antipasto salad, breaded beef tenderloin, and just a few cannolis. I figured if they did not like Italian food, they probably could not be trusted anyway. Oh, I gave them fruits and nuts too and some yogurt and stuff. They were great. If you have not heard them perform, I highly recommend it. That boy has some pipes. Problem was, after the band ate, David Phelps was ticked off at me because they wanted to take a nap instead of performing, but they all went back to the kitchen afterward to see if we had any leftovers.

While cooking was my passion, serving my Lord and Savior became my obsession. I wanted to live a life of purpose. I just did not see the point of seeking to fulfill the shallow goals and the temporary thrill of acquiring a new toy or possession day after day. There had to be more to life than that. I had always been a keen observer of other people. I liked to read biographies of successful people, but

87

even successful people were miserable. Multimillionaires accumulate more wealth because they could not consider themselves successful unless they were billionaires. When is enough, enough? Cheating and one-upmanship would lead to destroyed lives, broken marriages, massive divorce settlements, and the shattered hopes and dreams of the children of these ungodly unions. What would these children grow up to be?

I knew guys who lived quite simple lives, working meager jobs or starting their own small businesses. They worked with their families in these businesses, ate together at home, coached their kid's baseball or soccer teams, went to church together, honored God with their tithes, taught Bible studies, and went on the occasional mission trip to help less fortunate people. They were among the happiest people I know. On the other hand, I knew guys who were good at one point in their lives but sold out later. They let the success bug get to them and traded their principles for instant gratification in what I call the "look-at-me syndrome." They climbed the success ladder by stepping on or over countless people along their journey. They traveled the world; stayed in the very best hotels; ate at the finest restaurants; attended Super Bowls, World Series championship games, or Daytona 500 races; and had courtside seats at most NBA events, all the while lying to their family and friends about who they had been with the night before and using their friends to cover for their deceit. Most are probably vice president of this company or president of that company. Did you see me with this guy, or did you see my new fill in the blank? They look miserable. If you could talk to them when they let their facade down, they might even admit to the error of their ways and the bad choices they made. "It's too late now," they would reason. "I made my bed." This would usually follow the period of justification. "But you know," they would say, "I am a good guy. I believe in God. I even gave this amount to a charity before. I am a lot better than I use to be."

Most people just do not understand that it is not good enough to simply be good. Jesus said, "There is only one way to the Father, and it is through Me." An excellent book on this subject was written by Charles Stanley called *How Good Is Good Enough?* Matthew

19:23–26 states that "it is easier for a camel to crawl through the eye of a needle than for a rich man to enter the kingdom of God." Very true. However, I still believe in one of the last things Jesus said before He died on that cross for me and for you. As Jesus was nailed to the cross and hung between two criminals, one of them mocked Him, saying, "Save yourself and save us too." The other one said—I will paraphrase here—something like, "Shut up, fool! Don't you fear God even when you have been sentenced to die? We deserve to die for our deeds, but this man has not done anything wrong." Then he said to Jesus, "Master, remember me when you come into your kingdom." Jesus replied, "I assure you, *this day* you will be with me in paradise."

Was it because he was a good guy? Was it because he knew Jesus's name? No. It was because he knew the truth, he admitted that he was a sinner, and he believed that Jesus was Lord who was freely giving up His life for him and for the forgiveness of his sins. He asked Jesus to remember him when Jesus came into His kingdom. That is why he was forgiven and why I hold out hope for all those who have mocked the Lord in their own ways. They will see the errors of their ways before it is too late. They will repent and seek His face. My world was filled with guys like this. Good guys looking good on the outside, but on further inspection, are rotten and hollow on the inside. I was one of those guys. I knew I was created for something more than this. Was it too late for me? Had I allowed the rot inside me to grow for too long? Was there anything left the Lord could use to work with in me? I was on my knees in prayer, pleading with the Lord.

When Sunday morning came, Jinny and I went to church. I have no idea what the pastor was talking about. I was just sitting there, lost in thought, and flipping through my Bible. I was led to the book of 1 Chronicles chapter 4. While this book was about the ancestry of the nation of Israel, not exactly a captivating reading, I came across verse 9 about a man named Jabez who was more honorable than any of his brothers. His mother named him Jabez because his birth had been so painful. He prayed to the God of Israel, "Oh, that you would bless me and expand my territory! Please be with me in all that I do and keep me from all trouble and pain." God granted him his request.

This capsulized all that I was feeling. I read this over and over in such a heartfelt way. *Please, God, expand my territory. Give me something worthwhile to do for You, something worthwhile to live for and even die for if necessary.* Now I need to issue a warning here. This prayer is no joke. If prayed with a repentant attitude and a sincere heart, this prayer can change the course of your life. It did mine.

When the service was over, we got up and started heading toward the exit. An older guy named Louie Morabito, who was a Sunday school teacher, was standing in the hallway. I attended Louie's class several times. While I leaned a lot from him, he seemed to always be at odds with the senior pastor I felt really close to. We had locked horns on this topic several times, sometimes pretty emotionally. I nodded at Louie as we got to the door. He tapped on my shoulder and asked me if I would be willing to take a ride with him the following Sunday.

Now I do not know how many of you know much about the Italian culture. When an Italian wants to take you for a ride, it is not always a good thing. I hesitated and asked, "Where to?" He said, "Jackson State Prison." It was Michigan's maximum security prison. I said, "Louie, I spent a lifetime trying to stay out of that place. Now you want me to go for a Sunday visit?" Apparently, Louie had been going to Jackson and all the Michigan jails and prisons for over forty years, teaching Bible studies and holding services. He said that during the church service earlier, the Holy Spirit instructed him to reach out to me and ask me to join him.

Now how could I say no? I just asked the Creator of the universe to widen my territory and use me for His purposes. But prison? The renegotiation began. I thought that I was better suited for an advisory position than a foot soldier in the army of God—advising God, that is. I had a lifetime of experience telling Him how He should be doing things already. If I were in authority, I probably would have fired me before I even began. Apparently, He saw something I did not. In anticipation of the following Sunday, I was on my knees again. *Lord, I will go. I will walk through hell for You, but please, Lord, I beg of you, do not make me work with pedophiles. I just don't know if I could do this. How do I show the love of Your Son Jesus Christ to people I despise so much?*

I do not know how many of you have ever had the experience of being in the prison system, either as an inmate, a minister, or even as a visitor. It is extremely hard to explain because it is such a fluid feeling. It started with the dehumanization of the entire process. Background checks had to made in advance of my initial arrival, followed by the surrender of every personal item that I had carried for years and years, including belts, wallet, all currency, combs, keys, loose change, and a pocketknife. My Bible had to be examined, turned over, and shaken to check for any illegal communication or contraband. This all was done before walking through a metal detector, followed by a guard with a wand who would check everywhere on your person…and I mean *everywhere.* The pat down followed as I entered the next little holding chamber where I just knew that eyes were looking me over, checking for any behavior issues I may be expressing. Was I overly nervous? Was I just imagining this step of the process? I could not honestly say. The guard would say, "Open on three, close on two." The automatic doors would slide, and the sounds of heavy metal reinforced steel would clang shut.

All freedom I had taken for granted in my entire life had been left behind. I now found myself clutching my Bible, accompanied by Louie and another guard, and walking across the gigantic open prison yard surrounded by razor-sharp barb-wired-topped fences amongst hundreds of prisoners dressed in orange jump suits. I felt like if looks could kill, I would have been dead a hundred times on this walk across the yard. Guys were congregated in groups in several different areas. One area was a rather attractive vegetable garden. Another had an outdoor workout area with weights. There were a few basketball courts and a running track that had guys jogging and stretching. We were led to a small building at the very center of the yard where the chapel was.

As we approached, the sound of the most beautiful music was drifting through the air, praise and worship music. The guard opened a door with his keys, and we were let in. What happened next blew my mind. About 120 inmates were all sitting on rows of benches as excellent musicians played very upbeat praise music. Everything came to a stop amid shouts of joy as they saw their pastor enter the room.

Louie Morabito was a legend in the prison system. I have never seen a congregation of believers before or since that showed the kind of love these men showed Louie on this day or every other day that I accompanied him there. Louie walked up to the lectern and began the service by reciting prayers he had led thousands of times before as evidenced by all the inmates reciting them from memory right along with him. He spoke to them with a boldness that you seldom see preached from the pulpits in churches all over the country. More importantly, he told them the truth in love with the authority of God Himself. After several minutes, he introduced me as his good friend to the congregation. He told them that he had been inspired by the Holy Spirit to invite me to come with him today and give my testimony to them. They graciously applauded. The problem was, Louie never told me that he wanted me to share my testimony.

I was stunned. I must have looked like a deer stuck in the headlights of a truck. I had never done it before in my life. I turned my back to the group and sent up an emergency prayer for help. *Lord, please give me the words that these guys need to hear from You, not me.* I turned it over to Him. I walked up to the lectern and began to speak. I told them my story. Not from someone who was looking down at them for where they were but from the point of being an equal. I told them if it were not by the grace of God, I should be sitting in their seat and they could be talking to me. I told them if it were not for the prayers of my mother, grandmother, and sisters, I would be serving time too. It was as simple as taking a right turn instead of a left that the cops arrested other guys, not me. I told them that it was not until I turned my whole life over to my Jesus that things began to change for me. I still considered myself a practicing Christian. I had not made it yet. I needed their prayers. I showed them the Bible I carried with me, but I also usually carry a .40-caliber side arm in my waistband. When confronted with bad dudes, I would tell them I preferred to share about my Jesus, but if they persisted in their bad intentions toward me or one of my family members, I would have no problem introducing them to Jesus face-to-face. That one brought the house down. They knew I still needed prayers.

My testimony must have been effective as grown men were sobbing. When Louie asked if any of them would like to follow Christ, fifteen guys came up to the altar and asked me to pray for them with the prayer of salvation. I have never felt so fulfilled and blessed. The Creator of the entire Universe had chosen me to bring His message of salvation, and because of my obedience that day, fifteen souls would be spending eternity with the Lord forever. I found my new church. They asked me to come back, which I did every week, sometimes twice a week, for the next twelve years.

As we got ready to leave the chapel, a guy came up and asked if he could have a word with me in private. He asked me if I was from the Detroit area. I said yes. "The east side around the suburbs of St. Clair Shores near Grosse Point area?" When I confirmed it, he went on to say, "You don't remember me, but I remember you. I cut you off with my car. You and I had words that led to me getting out of my car and threatening to kick your butt. You also got out of your car. We kicked each other's butts. I had real anger issues then," he said (as if I didn't), "it led to me getting sentenced here for fifteen years." He was the mirror image of who I was at that time in my life.

We both embraced each other and openly cried. God just sent this man as confirmation that what I just shared with the inmates was true and from Him.

But for the Grace of God Go I!!!

18

The Difference a Good Bible Makes

By 2009, Jennifer Granholm was the governor of Michigan. The prison system in Michigan was in turmoil, as was the rest of the state. Morale among prison guards and administrators was at an all-time low. They called her the Queen of the Quick Fix. The state of Michigan was almost broke so funding was slashed from every department. The only people who were happy were the inmates. Career criminals were being released into the streets to satisfy line-item cuts in the department of corrections. Rapists, murderers, or pedophiles—it did not matter. The inmates laughed at the guards, and the police who put their lives on the line to apprehend some of these really bad guys. The court systems cost taxpayers hundreds of millions of dollars to make sure everyone got their day in court. The probation department were tasked with the re-entry system of slowly letting these offenders get reintroduced into society, all the while keeping an eye on them to try and insure that no more inno-cents would fall prey to some of their devious ways. If John Q public would have only known what was going on in their government. It was a part of the process that required released inmates to undergo a series of classes on how to re-assimilate into society as well as their new responsibilities in this society. I knew this was because the guys had to be excused from our Bible studies to attend these classes, requiring a bunch more forms and permission slips. They would barely be gone from class long enough to walk across the yard and back. They had to sign a document as proof that they attended all of these classes. Some cared enough to stop by just to say good-bye and thank us for everything.

There were some guys I was happy for, like Mr. Johnston. His story hit me really hard. From time to time, we would ask one of our long-term attendees to share their stories on how they came to know the Lord as their Savior. His story would help to shape my life story in years to come. His story started out when he was just a teenager. He did not even know his parents. He was out one night with a couple of guys, and they were getting high. He had a couple of joints on him as he was entrusted to hold their stash. The police grabbed them, frisked them, and found their drugs. According to Mr. Johnston, their stash was just over the minimum for the prosecutor to charge him with possession with intent to deliver. He was given a court-appointed attorney who negotiated a settlement. If he were to plead guilty, avoiding a trial, he would get the prosecutor to drop the intent to deliver charge. He would only have to spend five days in the county jail or pay the fine. Since Mr. Johnston had no money at all and no one even cared about his predicament, he would serve the five days.

On his first night in jail, he was visited by a big guy who he called Bubba. Bubba forcibly raped him. On the second night, Bubba came back with another guy. They both raped him repeatedly throughout the night. No one listened to his pleas for help. On the third night, when Bubba came back, Mr. Johnston managed to get a shiv, a homemade knife. He repeatedly stabbed Bubba in self-defense. He was charged and convicted of attempted murder and was sentenced to fifteen years in prison. While in prison you now were forced to make a choice of what gang you were going to become a part of just stay alive, he made the wrong choice. The guys he hooked up with were led by two guys doing double life sentences for murder. They decided one day that they had enough of their prison life and planned an escape. During the process, a guard was killed. Because Mr. Johnston was a known member of this gang, they were all charged with murder and given life sentences. This all started with smoking one joint and a broken criminal justice system that processed kids like they were of no value at all. When some people try to say that this is a harmless vice, I wish they could hear Mr. Johnston's story. Even after enduring all off this, he thanked God for forgiving him. Mr. Johnston asked Jesus to take control of his life. He was now over seventy years old.

Several years earlier at one of our Bible studies, Mr. Johnston admired my Bible. He had with him an old Gideon Bible that was worn, but more from just carrying it around than reading it. He said he had trouble with the King James Version because of its use of the old English text. Since he barely went to grade school, it was difficult for him to read. The Bible that I used regularly was an NIV Life Application Study Bible. It was marked up with notations or else I would have given it to him. I told him I would get him one of his own. I checked with the warden and found that it was quite the process to get any reading material into the prison. I reasoned that I might as well buy a whole case of these Bibles and submit them for the intake process if I was going to do any at all. It took two weeks. When I carried a case of Bibles into our Bible study, I got mobbed. Guys were acting like it was Christmas morning. They were begging for one of the dozen Bibles in the case. I gave one to Mr. Johnston and handed out the rest on a first-come, first-serve basis. These Bibles cost me about seventy bucks apiece, and everyone wanted one. I began researching where I could purchase these Bibles for a better price. I found a bookstore whose owner agreed to partner with me and give us these Bibles at around $25. He also had an engraving machine. In honor of my mentor Louie Morabito, I had Louie's name engraved on all the Bibles we purchased. Jinny and I were not supporting a local church at this time so we made the prison ministry our church. Over the years, we bought and distributed hundreds of these Bibles.

While some thought of these Bibles as gifts, I explained to them that they should regard them as tools. Workers could not work properly without the right tools, after completing our initial three-week Bible study we would award them with certificates of completion as well as a new autographed Bible. The Bible studies instantly tripled in size. The chaplain had to cut off requests for guys to come to our classes, and we had to move to a larger facility. While the Bible studies became extremely popular and the guys were getting a lot out of the classes evidenced by the number of guys giving their hearts to Jesus, requests to be baptized were growing and growing. Our God has a way of keeping us humble.

A couple of the lifers, who were regular attendees of our classes, stayed behind one day to talk to us. They felt we were being used. In the prison system, everything of value was used in their barter system. *Everything.* Some guys were showing up just to get our Bibles so they could trade them on the open market for as little as an extra candy bar or coffee. The guys were ticked off, but Louie nearly came unglued. He was going to tell all of them off next week because he knew the cost of these Bibles. After the initial shock, I thought about the great God we serve and how He just humbled us on our ride home that day. I began to laugh, which infuriated Louie all the more. I then told Louie that it was all in how we chose to look at the situation. While humbling us, God also found a way for those Bibles to end up in the right hands. Someone who valued them more than the recipient had given up something of value just to get their hands on one of our Bibles. God *is* great!

On the morning of May 25, 2009, I woke up, made a pot of coffee, and retrieved my morning copy of the *Detroit Free Press*. What I read sent shock waves through to my very soul and changed the direction of my life forever. In our culture today, there are so many sick acts perpetuated by people against children. This story really got to me. A five-year-old girl had gone missing in the town of Monroe, Michigan. Her name was Neveah Buchanan. The whole Monroe community turned out to look for this little girl. I do not know if I have ever been to Monroe, but my heart broke for this community. News reports came daily as the search continued and widened. I prayed for this little girl and the entire community every day. A couple of weeks later, a family of fishermen were fishing along the banks of the River Raisin when they found Little Nevaeh's body covered in crude cement. The autopsy results found dirt in Nevaeh's lungs. She had been buried alive. Her family and all of us were left to imagine the horrors Neveah experienced in her last moments alive. The

Monroe County sheriff never made an arrest. The two suspects with ties to Neveah's mom, were registered sex-offenders and had been recently released from the Michigan Department of Corrections. One had served fifteen years for multiple criminal sexual misconduct convictions. Her murder was never solved.

I felt violently sick. I have always wondered out loud how these politicians and bureaucrats sleep at night or if they even care about how their actions affect other people and families, especially the little defenseless children of God. I knew there was nothing I could do for Nevaeh, she was now resting in the arms of Jesus. I resolved to spend the rest of my life trying to help keep another family, another community, and another child of God from having to experience the kind of pain Neveah endured. I look forward to the day I get to meet you in paradise, my little angel. Your life was not in vain. If I could make a difference in the life of even one wayward soul that could inflict this kind of pain on my family or your family, it would have been a life well spent.

While I continue to serve in the prison ministry, I heard a call from my Lord to reach younger guys who had been abandoned, abused, and neglected by the system. Once these youngsters ended up in the prison system, it was almost too late. There is little truth to the concept of rehabilitation in the system. What happens is more likely for the prisoners to get master's degrees in crime and getting caught up in the revolving door of arrest and release. I informed Louie that I would continue to assist him in the Morabito prison ministries, however, I would also be starting a new ministry. Louie was disappointed. He hoped that I would eventually take over his ministry, but he prayed with me for direction from our Lord for both of us and our ministries.

19

My World Gets Rocked... Again (2009)

Things were going well now in most areas of my life. The business was running as smooth as could be expected. My marriage was as solid as it ever had been. Oh, there were plenty of challenges in the family, but that was a constant. I was learning about Jesus. He was getting to be more and more important to me. I had prayed for mentors and He blessed me in so many ways.

I was new at this church business, and it is a business. Bill's, revenue, and business practices are things I was good at since I had owned and operated businesses most of my life. I found out that pastors and for the most part church leadership had no idea of what it took to run a business. Making sound business decisions were not in their vocabulary. Just because the lead pastor may be a good teacher, preacher, or inspirational speaker did not make him or her a good business manager. Even Jesus saw this when He gathered His apostles. He included a tax guy (Matthew) and someone to watch the purse strings (Judas), which the irony is not lost on us seeing what happened with him. As is the case with many successful businesses, competition and territorial infighting takes place. I guess that is why they try and teach kids at a young age to color within the lines. When they stray outside of their boundaries, things get messy. It only gets worse as these children get older and become men and women. They get more and more territorial and entrenched in their definitions of right and wrong.

I was blessed to meet and study under the tutelage of many wonderful, knowledgeable men of God. When I was with them, I felt like I was given the opportunity to study at the feet of the apostles themselves. Three of these men stood the test of time and taught me many values that I carry with me to this day. Their testimonies were incredible. One brother in the Lord, Bob, had lost his son to cancer. The day after he buried His only son, he washed his face, put on his best suit, and came to church to worship and give thanks to his Lord and Savior, Jesus Christ. This would have destroyed other men, but Bob stood on his faith and continues to serve his Lord. The other man was elderly, and I enjoyed taking him to his appointments and just spending time with him. He sent his beloved wife home to be with the Lord several years before I met him. He enjoyed my company and my cooking. I would bring him meals all the time and arranged to have meals sent to him from his favorite restaurant after I moved away. While traveling with him one day, I asked Mr. Tony a question if he happened to have a Bible handy. He said yes. I did not see it with him so I asked him where it was. He pointed to his brain, indicating he could quote the entire Bible. It blew me away.

Louie Morabito was more than this to me. He became my mentor, my confidant, my confessor, my teacher, my big brother, and my best friend. I loved the man, and I am not afraid to admit it. I grew very protective of Louie. I hated to see him hurt or sad. He taught me how to love unconditionally. He taught me how to love the unlovable and how to find the Christ in anybody. He taught me how to stay steadfast in the face of the strongest opposition and how to stay the course that the Lord puts you on, no matter how long the journey is or how uphill and twisted the road becomes. He taught me to seek only the approval of the one who had chosen me to do the task that I alone was given. He insisted that the praise of mere mortals was useless, that it was better to hear the words of the Master ("Welcome home, my good and faithful servant") than the platitudes of people who would praise you today but throw you under the bus tomorrow. He taught me to watch out for the wolves who come in sheep's clothing. I accompanied this man for close to twelve years as he brought God's word to prisoners all over Michigan. The travel time was some of the most enjoyable for us. I learned so much. He did this with little or no financial support from his church. I could not understand why the leadership would seldom, if ever, recognize his work. I watched firsthand in just those twelve of his sixty-year ministry how people gave their lives over to the Lord, be baptized, and recommit themselves to God more than all the churches I have attended combined. I actually felt like we were walking into Satan's very own home and reclaiming souls for Jesus. This task is not for everyone. It took a special type of person for this work.

During this same time period, I watched the leadership of our church fly their entire families to foreign lands, pay all the expenses, come back home, and speak for weeks about a flower garden they helped to weed. Oh, we would have to take special collections to pay for these mission trips. Being a businessman, I could not see the wisdom in this. Why didn't we just send a couple hundred dollars to the local pastor, wherever they were going, and have them pay some locals to weed flowers? We could have given the rest of the money to Louie's ministry. The return on investment of souls saved would be exponentially more worthwhile. But what did I know! Being new to the faith, my big mistake was I chose to place these men on a pedestal. I stood in awe of them and their level of knowledge in God's word. All good men with good intentions, but they were fallible men just the same. It was not a matter of if these men would eventually disappoint or fail me one way or another, it was a matter of when. When they slipped, stumbled, or even fell from that lofty perch I placed them on, they crumbled, and I would be crushed. It was not their fault. They had not asked to be placed in those lofty places, but they failed me just the same. In some cases, worse than others.

In the case of church leadership, I found the best explanation from the commentary of one of my Bibles. "Many leaders and authorities today demand allegiance, some of whom would even have us turn from Christ to follow them. When they seem to know the Bible, their influence can be dangerously subtle. They are modern-day false teachers. How can you recognize false teachers?

1) They teach what is contrary to the truth found in the Scripture.
2) They promote trivial and divisive controversies instead of helping people come to Jesus.
3) They are not concerned about personal evidence of God's presence in their lives, spending time on meaningless discussions instead.
4) Their motivations are to make a name for themselves.

To protect yourselves from the deception of false teachers, learn what the Bible teaches and remain steadfast in your faith in Christ alone. My final straw came after a Wednesday evening service where an associate pastor played a movie by the German evangelist Reinhard Bonnke, which showed a rescue ship (a metaphor for the church) that was equipped with many life rafts, life jackets, and staffed for life-saving missions out in very rough seas. After receiving a SOS message and orders from the navy to rescue the passengers of an overturned vessel nearby, the occupants of this "church" just kept partying and talking about their vast experience in modern life-saving techniques and whose methods would work best as the victims drowned. At the end of the video, Reinhard asked, "Had your church become nothing more than a cruise ship or was it the kind of emergency vessel needed to save souls God intended it for?"

I raised my hand and waited to be called on. I stood up and proclaimed that we had just witnessed what had become of our church. I asked why were we not supporting ministries like Louie's that were producing so much fruit. A few of the church staff members came over and asked me to come with them. I was being called to the office. A few days later, several of the church deacons asked to meet with me. They said they wanted to hear me out. I was told at this meeting that the church board was going to have a meeting of reconciliation, which my wife and I were asked to attend.

At this meeting, I heard for the first time a new definition of *reconciliation*. If I would apologize to the senior pastor, who did not even bother attending this meeting, and to his head deacon, we would be allowed to stay in the congregation on probation. In other words, if I would repent, bow done, and kiss their rings, I would just go on double-secret probation. All this for having the audacity to stand up for another brother in the Lord. I looked over at my wife and asked her if she had seen enough yet. She said yes, and we left the church. It would not be the last church I would be asked to leave. I did not need a country club in a church. I needed Jesus. I am all about manning the lifeboats, not for going on a cruise.

20

Are You Going to Move When
I Tell You to Move?

Jinny and I continued to pray hard for a word from God. We wanted to find a good Bible-based church where we could feel productive. Many people, when looking for churches to attend, usually say that they are looking for a place to feel fed. We were looking for a place that we could help feed. We felt that we were no longer baby Christians that needed to be spoon-fed spiritual baby food. We were looking to get into the meat and potatoes of serving Christ. Some friends of ours invited us to attend their church. Things were looking fairly good. We were working in their ministries. Jinny was cutting hair for the homeless and I was helping out in the kitchen when we ran smack into one of our "nonnegotiables" as we called them.

I like things simple. I had brought my sister to a program that was examining how many denominations had more in common than differences. This one was going to examine the differences and similarities between Protestants and Catholics. My sister is a lifelong Catholic who loves the Lord and follows in the traditions that our family was raised in. I was more of a black sheep of the family. I needed to read for myself what was in God's instruction manual. The priests and nuns of my youth telling me that the Bible needed to be interpreted by someone smarter than me did not sit well. I know I am not the sharpest knife in the drawer, but compared to some of the leaders of the church, I could hold my own. So I began to search, and I am glad I did.

I asked my sister Julee to accompany me to this six-week study, and she obliged me. She could never say no to me. I was her baby brother, and she spoiled me rotten. When we arrived for the first week, there were about fifty people in the class. She was the only Catholic there. The class started out fairly smooth. By the second week, Julee was feeling a bit more comfortable. She glanced over at me when one particular fellow, who was somewhat involved with the church leadership previously, went on a rant, bashing Catholics. I spent more time defending most of the teachings of the Catholic faith once I left it than I ever did when I was still practicing it. Do not get too excited, I still had my misgivings, I just knew who their creator was also, and it was up to Him to judge, He had not abdicated that role over to me just yet. Instead of a meeting of the minds, it turned into a "Why my way of worshipping the Creator is right and your way is wrong."

There is a simple test that I use to guide my way. Jesus came to gather his flock. We have been encouraged from the beginning to have unity in the body of Christ. Jesus went so far to chastise the "so called religious" and said they were more in love with their religion and customs than God Himself. On the other hand, Satan come to lie, kill and destroy. The tool he uses is division in social status, black, white, red, yellow, political affiliations, and church denominations, on and on. Is our Sabbath on a Saturday or a Sunday? What does it matter? My Bible says, "All who call on the name of the Lord shall be saved." If this is not enough, I urge you to hold a newborn baby in your arms or sit with a retired military veteran in a nursing home and let him or her tell you of a life of service. Go to a funeral home where an elderly person is laying to rest their soul mate and facing an uncertain future for the rest of their days. Look into the faces of a young couple who have found love for the first time or how they are dealing with the senseless loss of their child. I guarantee you that in all of these cases, you will not think of what race they are, what denomination they practiced their religion, or who they voted for in the last election. You see, folks, hate and division is not something that our God created us with. It is the seeds that were planted in us by the adversary of this world who is all about hate and keeping us apart. While there is no such thing as a perfect church or a perfect anything, this place is not for us. We would move on.

The next week, we attended the church I was first saved in. As we sat there, listening to the message, Jinny looked over at me with a strange look on her face. I just heard something that was directed at us. After the service, when we made it back to our car, she asked me what had just happened in that service. I told her that I heard God say to us, "Are you going to move when I tell you to move?" Apparently, she heard the same message. What did this mean? What would He have us do? We prayed and told God we would go where He wanted us to go and serve Him in any manner He wanted us to.

The following week, I was home getting supper ready when the phone rang. When I answered it, it was Jinny calling from work. She asked, "Are you sitting down?" This was never a good sign. What happened now? These kinds of calls were usually followed by a code phrase that Jinny and I had that we learned from the book of James 1:2–4, "Consider it pure joy when you are faced with troubles of many kinds for the testing of your faith produces perseverance. Let perseverance finish its work so that you may be mature and complete, not lacking anything." When we were at work, we rarely had a minute to share together so when we walked by each other and when asked how the other was doing, our go to response was, "Consider it pure joy." This told the other that we were too busy dealing with problems to talk. This call was different though. There was something different in her voice. I sat down as instructed. She then proceeded to tell me that one of our part-time nail technicians asked to speak to her in the office. This young women informed Jinny that her father recently sold an exceptionally large business and bought another business to set his son up. Since he just had two children, she asked her dad what he planned on doing for her. When he asked her what she wanted to do, she replied that she always wanted to own her own day spa and salon. The father told her to inquire if her employers would be willing to sell their business to them.

I just about fell out of my chair. Businesses like ours seldom, if ever, sold. We did not own the building, and the value was in the good will of our customer base and our employees. This was

September, and by December, we completed the deal. Our business, which had taken us twenty years to build, was sold. We put our home up for sale then and planned on selling our property in Northern Michigan when we got up there in the spring. Whatever place sold first, we would live in the other. Our home downstate sold in two weeks, so we were on our way up to Harrisville, Michigan, a small town on the shores of Lake Huron.

Our families went crazy. They thought we were nuts. After all, neither one of us ever lived outside of the Metro Detroit area. Between the two of us, it seemed like we knew everyone there. I had connections and relationships galore. We had children, grandchildren, elderly parents, and siblings. How could we be so selfish? Neither one of us could explain, but we believed that God took over our decision-making. We swore that we would go where He told us to go, and we were never more sure of anything than this was of God. The ones in our family that did not have a relationship with the Lord just rejected us. The price for following Jesus is not cheap. You have to make sacrifices, which is not at all easy. The words of Jerry Lewis rang sharp in my mind, "For those who understand, no explanation is necessary. For those who do not understand, no explanation will suffice."

After being surrounded by people 24-7, we were in very uncharted territory. We did not even know if we liked each other that much. We had no mutual interests except for our desire to serve our Lord. We did not know a single soul in this whole community. We were alone.

It's always been about the family but the family
has grown by several hundred more now

21

Country Life

It is the spring of 2010, we are going to try our hand at this country life. Several years before Jinny and I moved to Harrisville, we rented a cottage on Lake Huron that allowed dogs. We always had golden retrievers. Most people who are owned by their dogs know that it is all about the dogs, vacations included. My wife even had me purchase a Chevy Avalanche because she said "the girls" they could no longer be called dogs because that was not human, so it was "the girls" or "the children." Our dogs, *the children*, got so spoiled that there were times when we had left them in the car to run into a store, we would find them sitting in the front seat upon returning. They would not budge and looked at us like, "I have this, Dad. Get in the back and let me drive." So we would sit in the back seat for a while just to see the expression on the faces of other people coming out of the store. It was hysterical. Can you tell we were bored by now and had to find ways to amuse ourselves?

Jinny would walk the girls on the beach for hours. She saw how low I was feeling after my latest heart procedure and suggested that I go to a real estate office in town and pick up some listing tickets on property for sale. "You always said that you wanted hunting property," she said. "Take a look around. Maybe in a few years, we will be in a position to buy some."

It sounded good to me, even though I knew she was just politely blowing me off and wanted to get rid of me for the day. In my travels, I ended up going down a one-way street. These one-way streets in the country could go for miles with the houses sometimes miles

109

apart from the nearest neighbor. Talk about solitude. I came across an eighty-acre parcel with a single-wide old trailer on it. This property had a giant pine tree right in the front yard and a mud hole that was supposed to be a pond. In years to come, we would make most of the important decisions in our life under the upstretched arms of that pine tree. We named it our decision tree. I began to haggle with the owner (Italians never pay the asking price for anything. When someone says they are asking X for something, they have established their starting point, and you counter with Y. Now Y totally depends on how unreasonable the other guy's X was. The give and take could go on for weeks or days, depending on how easy or hardheaded the parties are until you settle on a price. If you felt, based on your knowledge of the value of whatever you are haggling over, that you were on the right side of the deal, you would have a bargain, and the matter would be settled right then.

This was just a long-winded way of telling you and, more importantly, Jinny, that I had gotten a bargain. She was now the proud owner of eighty acres of prime hunting land. That would also teach her not to blow me off again and leave me alone for too long. I could tell that she approved when I brought her to walk the property when she said, "I can do this. But I have to ask you, what part of 'in a few years' did you not understand? Secondly, do not think, under any circumstances, you will get me to live up here." On May 1, 2010, we moved into our new home out in the backwoods of Harrisville, Michigan, two hundred miles north of everyone we knew and loved. And it was her idea!!! It was also God's plan for our lives. It would be 550-mile round-trip commute to meet Louie at Jackson every week, but I did ask God to widen my territory, and I meant it. Problem was, I was clueless on how He planned on using us up here.

Before we got too deep into this country living, Jinny and I decided to celebrate our retirement by taking a trip. Jinny started scouring travel brochures. When I came home, she was beaming. She found the perfect trip for us to go on. The problem was, it was overseas. I never had a desire to leave the USA. I had nightmares of my time spent in Quebec and did not want to go through that again. "No, wait!" she proclaimed. "It is a cruise, and one of the stops is in

Rome and then Sicily, where your grandparents are from. The itinerary includes going to most of the places Christ was at in Israel and where His three-year ministry took him. We are actually going to walk in the footsteps of Jesus and the apostles!"

That part got me excited. The Italy part, however, I did not know what their statute of limitations were or if they held grudges from one generation to another. The stories I heard about some of my grandparents and their families…well, things could get dicey. My whole life, people asked me questions like what town my grandparents were from in Sicily and if I ever went there to visit, almost like it was some kind of sacrilege to not go there on a pilgrimage or something. My reply was always the same, "If it was so great there, then why did all those *dagos* come over here?" Boy, was I wrong! It was the single best trip of both of our lives. No words could describe the feelings of standing at Jesus's birthplace and being baptized again in the River Jordan. We could almost hear him preaching on the shores of Galilea to the five thousand when he fed them with a few loafs of bread and some fishes. We were kneeling and praying at the same rock at the mount of Transfiguration as the apostles slept under the olive trees. Walking down the Via Delarosa, we could almost hear the pain of Mary as she watched her beloved son carry a wooden cross to His death. We travelled all over and visited spots that are in the news and history books. When we see or hear them now, it takes on a new meaning because we were there. I could not get enough of Jesus who died for me on that cross. My Jesus.

When the cruise ship docked into the port in Sicily, I reacted in a way that I never expected. My first sight of this beautiful place took my breath away, and I began to weep openly. To think that my grandparents gave all of this up. They left everything they knew and loved to seek a better future for me and future generations to come. I was now eternally grateful for the sacrifice they made that, up until that moment, I had taken for granted. I send up a prayer of thanksgiving to all of my ancestors every time I think of that place. We were in Sicily for only one day. We were taken to a small four-acre farm that three female cousins had leased to try and make a living. Because of the lack of work on the island, their husbands had informed them that they too would be going in separate directions to seek work overseas. One was going to Australia, one to Canada, and one to the USA. They could not bear to be separated so they found this little spot and turned it into a tourist attraction of old-world Italy. They grew fruits and vegetables and processed the best olive oil I have ever tasted. One of the husbands built an outdoor oven where fresh breads and pastries were made daily. Sausages and cured hams hung from the overhead racks while barrels of wine fermented underneath. A cappuccino machine brewed fresh coffee.

We sat a table, sampling their fares and taking in the incredible smells of orange and lemon trees. A little glass of limoncello, a homemade wine, finished off the meal I will never forget. One of the sisters tended to the animals. The sheep, goats, and miniature donkeys that had a dark cross shape across their backs were fascinating to me. They were called Jerusalem donkeys. One of the ladies sat down with me and told me the legend of the Jerusalem donkey. It was said that while Jesus was led into Jerusalem on Palm Sunday, he told one of His disciples to go to a particular place where he would find a colt tied to a fence. "Tell the owner that the Master has need of it." They took the colt and placed Jesus on its back. As he was led into town, people lined up and laid palm branches on the ground in front of him. After Jesus was beaten and tormented, Jesus carried the cross to Golgotha to be nailed up to it and hung up to die. The little donkey followed the crowd up to the cross, unable to bear seeing the pain inflicted on His Jesus, so he turned his back to the cross. The shadow of the cross fell across the little animals back. From that day forward, all of its offspring would be born with the cross of Christ on its back.

When we got back to the States, we stopped at my sister's who was taking care of our golden retriever Sancho before heading home. My daughter Karen called me to tell me they decided to purchase a dog and went to a breeder in a town closer to our home. They put a $100 nonrefundable deposit on a new goldendoodle puppy but found another breeder who had one ready to come home so they had bought that one instead. The guy had one golden retriever puppy that Karen and the kids wanted us to have, and we could even apply the $100 to the costs. I tried to explain to her that a hundred bucks in the life of a puppy was like finding a penny on the floor. It was a huge commitment of time and money. The truth is, most people should not even consider having a pet if they cannot dedicate enough time and resources to the animal. I promised her we would stop and take a look, but I was making no promises. I would not be making any more snap decisions. I was going to think everything through.

We arrived at the breeder's ranch, the little puppy was right outside, looking at a pen of exotic birds. A couple of pens over was a pasture with horses and a Jerusalem donkey. He only had one, and it one was not for sale. I knew I had to have one on our new farm because they were also known as fierce defenders against coyotes, mountain lions, and other predators. I picked up the puppy and brought it to the truck to show Jinny. Sancho was not one bit amused. She was like, Okay, that is nice. Now lose the puppy and let's get going." Jinny loved the pup, but I told the owner I would think about it and get back to him. He told me if I change my mind, his older golden was going to be pregnant again so we could check back with him in a few months. I returned the pup to him and drove sixty miles home. As soon as we got into the house, I told Jinny to get back in the truck. Then I called the guy and told him I was on my way back for the pup. Jinny looked at me like I was an idiot. I said, "What? I told you no more snap decisions. Now I had to drive another 120-mile round trip in order to keep my promise. Promises are important." I told her.

When Sammy, the new addition to our family, saw me come back for her, she leaped into my arms. I fell in love. Sancho, on the other hand, not so much. She was aggravated. The looks she gave me were priceless. "This rug rat better not try to muscle in on my territory, and she is not getting any of my toys!" It only took a couple of weeks and they were best buddies, but Sancho was always skeptical of me from that day on. She had good reason to be.

The next week, I was on my way to pick out our newest additions to the family, a couple of Jerusalem donkeys I found in western Michigan. The woman I bought them from had about sixty of these donkeys all over the place. She had a barn and pastures, but the animals followed her into the whole lower level of her two-story colonial house. Two of the donkeys took a liking to Jinny and would not leave her side. I told her I would take them both. "It was not right for anything to be alone. They needed a friend," I reasoned. If you were going to feed one, what would it take to feed two?" What I did not consider was the other care they would need. Veterinarians who do house calls were not cheap. We found a great one in town I trusted more than any other doctors practicing in these parts. She was more dependable for sure, but she used up her one mistake early on in our relationship. She has been great ever since. They also needed to have pedicures every six to eight weeks. Did you know that animals needed pedicures? I did not. Their hoofs would grow so fast, it curls up and could make them lame. Our neighbor Sandy found us a local guy named Matt. He was a furrier, what they called guys who did this kind of work. He did not take kindly to me referring to him as my donkey's pedicurist. He was a great guy though. He could have stepped right out of a John Wayne movie or *Wagon Train* episode.

I was so happy. I was living the dream and serving the Lord; it does not get any better than this. Every day I would go out and do my chores and spend a good part of the day with my dogs and donkeys. I was always taking them out for treats. I loved to hear the donkeys get excited and make this god-awful noises that I grew to love when they saw me coming. We named them Sunday and Sara, but that would change sometimes daily, depending on who was coming over or who asked about them. I liked to mess with people, so if my buddies called, I told them their names were Chris and Bob, or when my brother-in-law, Harold, would come up, I would call them Harold and John; the names would change constantly. If I were challenged on why I named them after the person who was asking about them, I would respond that the donkeys reminded me of other jackasses I knew. It usually got a laugh. Not always.

Well, the joke was about to be on me. One day, I was bringing out the treats to the donkeys when I noticed that Sunday was significantly wider and heavier than Sara. *They were both females, so pregnancy was impossible*, I thought. We had gotten them about nine months before. I started reading up on the topic and began to freak out. I called my friend, the veterinarian, and asked if she could come out and check her out. I call Cathy Jo, the vet, my friend, not because we spend any time together but rather because I must have purchased her a new truck or two over the years with all these darn vet bills, and she better like me after all this. Well, anyways, she said she would send her assistant out tomorrow to examine the donkey. He arrived on schedule, examined her, and declared, "Yes, sir, you have a pregnant donkey, and she could deliver any time after this month." He told me she would need all kinds of prenatal vitamins and shots and for me to buy a special grain mixture to feed her. He said he would come back in a week or two to check on her. There went another couple of truck payments for the good doctor. Everyone was so excited. I was in full-blown panic mode. *How do I deliver a baby donkey? Who could I line up to help me? How would I know if there was a problem?* I began doing what any ignorant man with no experience around the birth of anything would do. I started gathering supplies. I needed hot water. *How would I heat the water in the barn?* I need blankets, bandages, extra lights, plastic gloves, a baby monitor, and books on the subject. I was a hot mess. Night after night, I would go out to the barn to check on her. Nothing. Weeks tuned into a month, still no baby. I was exhausted. I called Cathy Jo back.

"What the hell is going on?" I asked. Her assistant told me that their gestation period could be up to thirteen months. I told her I would not live that long. She agreed to come out herself by the first of the next week if she had not delivered by then. (She knew I was a nutcase by the way I treated all of my dogs.) Her assistant had quit and did not even give her a notice, so she was running behind. I waited and waited, and the next Tuesday, Cathy Jo showed up with the newer truck (I told you I am sure I bought that for her), and she accompanied me out to the barn. She pulled on a pair of super long rubber gloves and positioned herself behind Sunday and reached in as far as her arm would go.

She pulled her arm out, looked at me with a small grin on her face, and said, "I am sorry, Frank, it appears that all you have is a fat ass."

Just a Fat Ass

Now, I have been told that before, but never in this type of situation. My family, friends, and neighbors have never let me live this down.

But we were not done. Another younger couple had moved in down the road apiece. They had two children earlier in life who already left home, but they were blessed with another child later on. The mom had been diagnosed with multiple sclerosis. Things were not easy for her, but she is an angel. Her husband was seldom home since he raced dirt bikes and went to races all over the place. Her father who owned the home next door moved them to the house so they would be closer to him. That is about the only nice thing I can say about this guy. He set rules that they were not to call him after a certain time at night no matter what. How ridiculous. I told her she could call me 24-7 if she needed anything. She had a fighting spirit and no quit in her as she fought this dreadful disease like nothing I had ever seen since my late wife Julie's battle with cystic fibrosis. They were over the house all the time.

The little girl named Maddie had fiery red hair that matched her personality. She would just pop in to visit and was always helpful around the farm. She took to the donkeys right away and encouraged me to buy a cart because she wanted to train them to pull her around the property. She was great at it too. However, her real dream was to have her own horse. Her mother Sandy had a horse growing up. Those stories resonated with Maddie. They could not afford one and her grandfather wouldn't help at this point. Like I said, I already used up the one nice thing I had to say about him. I told Maddie to start looking for a horse if it was all right with her mom, but we needed two because I did not want them to be alone. Sandy called and, as was her style, started apologizing about Maddie's desire to have a horse. "Are you sure?" she asked. "I would not have offered if I was not sure, Sandy." She said, "Well, okay, I think we found a place on the other side of the state that had several horses for sale." She brought over some photos. We started planning to travel over to see them. "How would we know if these horses are healthy or sound? I asked the pedicurist—darn I mean, furrier to come with us. He said he would be glad to accompany us. Maddie was so excited.

What I did not know was Gramp's got wind of our plans and bought Maddie a horse himself. Good for her. There were many horses to choose from, we told them we were looking for gentler horses that would be good with kids and old people. I was also going to need a rather large horse, like a Budweiser Clydesdale, if it was going to carry me. They saddled up two beautiful horses. The first one was a bit spunky. Maddie rode it and nixed it. The next one was a brown quarter horse that Jinny attempted to get up on. Her foot slipped in the stirrup, and she ended up laying across the back of the horse like she had been shot and was being brought back on a pack-horse. Poor Matt, the furrier, tried to catch her, but his options were limited. He choose not to grab Jinny by her rear end and boost her up. He backed off.

The next horse they brought out was massive. I felt like I needed an elevator to get up on the thing. Not to be outdone, I got my foot in the stirrup and began to pull myself up without checking the cinch. The saddle slipped with me still hanging on slid under the horse. The horse let out a scream that startled everyone. Matt, Sandy, and Maddie stared in shock. Matt said, "I have been around horses for over forty-five years and I never heard a sound like that come out of one yet." I said, "I thought you knew about horses. That was horse speak for 'Get the hell off of me and let me ride you!'" "Frank, have you ever ridden a horse before?" he asked. He was not reassured when I said, Heck yes! I had spent an entire quarter riding the penny horse in front of Woolworths when I was a kid."

At this time, he tried to get us to just buy a couple sawhorses made of wood so nothing would get hurt. I did not take his advice. Maddie chose a beautiful white Arabian and another gorgeous brown quarter horse. We named them Stormy and Sampson. I would find out the locals had a few names for us downstaters, that being one of them. When they referred to us as being green, they meant that we were clueless on how things needed to be done. I believe they meant a deeper, darker shade of green when they spoke about me. I had a hard time trying to figure out what side of a screwdriver to use.

I saw a guy driving down the main highway in a dump truck hauling a bulldozer; his name is Ted. I tracked him down and hired him to put some trails in our woods. He wanted to know where I wanted him to put them in, but I did not have a clue. I took him to where the previous owner told me our property line was and told him our property was a quarter mile wide and half a mile deep. "Start on one corner and stay within those boundaries." I found out that nobody ever surveyed the property. I just put a trail through my neighbor's property on one side while the guy on the other side was playing me for a fool and had five acres of my land fenced in for himself. I just wanted to live peacefully but unwittingly started a range war. In my defense, these folks were different. When I get the opportunity to talk to one of the locals, and I ask for directions to anywhere. The conversation would go something like this, "You take this road down to old forty-one, turn left, and go down to where the three big oaks are on the corner of whatchamacallit road. Turn east and go by old man Fowler's place and continue till you get to Poor Farm Road. Head north until you get to the big rock next to the Old Stone Church. Take that road down to the lake. It's simple." It is scary because when people talk like that now, I know where they are sending me.

I also decided that I wanted to try planting a garden. I had a guy dig out the big mud hole and put in a fishing pond. It was something else I got to check off my bucket list. My mother Rose loved to fish but was deathly afraid of the water. I promised her when I was a young boy that when I grew up, I was going to build her a fishing pond stocked with fish. Mission accomplished. The excavator guys dug the pond fourteen feet deep to accommodate the fish and piled all the white clay up in the back clearing they had created. They spread it out nicely, creating a nice pasture. I went to work planting corn, beans, pumpkins, carrots, cabbages, and any other plants I could get my hands on. Did you know that you cannot even grow weeds in white clay soil? I didn't. The neighbors would come by, go home, and call friends to come over and look at how stupid their new neighbor was. They would laugh until their sides hurt. I was not done though. There was no quit in me. Some of these locals were not exceedingly kind and would look for ways to take advantage of strangers. You had to keep your guard up or you would end up paying several times the value of putting in a new well like me. What did I know about wells? I thought you just turned the handle at the sink and water appeared. Evidently not. I had a guy wanting to charge me over $6,000 just to grade my dirt in the front of my house.

I left one morning and headed into the big town of Alpena and came home with a delivery truck following me with my brand-new John Deere tractor. *I would do this job myself.* I thought. I had never driven a tractor before, but it could not be that hard. It had all the attachments, including a dump bucket, high-low forks, a grader, and a backhoe. Jinny came outside and just looked on in disbelief. "Leave it to you, my genius husband, just so you don't have to pay six thousand to get the job done by someone who knows what they're doing. Then you go out and spend thirty thousand on a machine you don't know how to operate." We laughed.

It would not be the only crazy or reactionary purchase I would make. I was determined to make this tractor work for me. I talked to another neighbor and told him that I wanted to put in an apple orchard. He said he knew a guy who knew a guy who could get me a deal on apple trees. "Now you're talking!" I found someone who could speak my language. He asked how many I wanted. I told him I would start with a dozen, two of each different kind. He said he would call me when he got them. I was on the job. I got my backhoe out and started digging large holes to accommodate the root balls of these trees. I had them all set. I was pretty pleased with myself, operating this backhoe and all. I needed to go downstate for a few days. While I was down there, my neighbor Neil called me and told me my trees were at his house but he was leaving for a couple days. If I would pick them up, he would have them next to his pole barn. I had my brother-in-law Harold coming back up north with his brother John. They would help me load the trees and plant them. As I arrived back home, I hooked up my trailer. We got in the truck and went over to Neil's. I told them to stay in the truck until I located the trees. Then we could pull up close to them so we would not have to carry them too far. I can still see the looks on their faces and the sounds of roaring laughter as I came walking back around the pole barn with all twelve trees in my left hand. It looked like I was carrying a bunch of asparagus spears. I guess I should have inquired about the size of these trees. It took me eight years, but those trees are now fifteen feet high. We are enjoying beautiful apples from the eight that survived.

I was not done either. Another neighbor Jinny met while walking our dogs got into a predicament. His brother-in-law had a company that was working on a giant oil spill in the Gulf of Mexico. He needed Rick to help him make large booms that floated on the sea to keep the oil together until it could be cleaned up. Rick had a bunch of chickens that needed tending while he was gone for a few months.

I opened my big mouth and told Rick I would do it. I told him that I was kicking the idea around of getting some chickens myself the following year, so this would give me some practice when I would start looking into building a chicken coop. The next day, Rick was over at my house. We were off to the lumberyard. Fifteen hundred dollars later, I ended up with a chicken palace, not a coop. He never had to leave for New Orleans after all.

I found myself in the chicken-raising business. I went to the feed store and fell into the next phase of this trap. If you buy the bags of chicken feed from them, they will give you six chickens for every bag you buy. I told the little old lady I would take six of this kind and six of that kind, thinking I was getting twelve chicks. They sent a boy out to the truck with twelve bags of feed and seventy-two chicks. I took six turkeys and a dozen ring-necked pheasants too. The pheasants lasted two days. They were so small that they ran right through the fencing out into the woods. The turkeys grew up so big that they weighed in over fifty pounds apiece dressed. We could not fit them in a normal oven. The chickens, well, did you know that when they reach a certain age, they lay an egg every day. I didn't. We had eggs coming out of our ears. Did you know that there are chickens that lay eggs that are already dyed for Easter eggs? I didn't. We had eggs of all sizes, shapes, and pastel colors. We were eating so many eggs during breakfast, lunch, and dinner that I would have needed a special meter to determine my cholesterol levels. The dogs were also eating eggs. I was ready to pay people to take the eggs. I made a sign and told people they were Sicilian eggs. I told people when they asked what a Sicilian egg was, that they came from Italian chickens that had an attitude.

One day, I get a call from my niece Julee. She was an elementary school teacher who was doing an experiment with her kids in class. They had eggs in an incubator that were ready to hatch. She told the kids she would find them a good home with her Uncle Frank. She knew I could never say no to her so I said just bring them up. Thank God that only four of them hatched. The kids named them Huey, Louie, Dewey, and Bob. Bob was the only chicken, while the rest were ducks. Oh, lucky me! Now I had to build a pond for the ducks.

These little guys stuck together like glue. They followed each other around and tried to stay away from the rest of the animals. When I put in the little pond for the duck, Bob discovered he was not a duck. When the first three jumped into the water, Bob followed them but immediately shot out of there like a cannon. Poor thing. My niece is still laughing.

What a mess they make too! Jinny wanted nothing to do with them. "They are disgusting," she would say. When I had to travel to the prison, Jinny was left with caring for the animals. When she went out to the palace to gather eggs one day, the wind blew the door shut, locking her inside. She was livid. Thank God she had her cell phone with her. She called the neighbor to come down and let her out. The gossip spread extremely fast in this small town. Everyone knew that there would be hell to pay when I got home. She called me as I was just entering the prison and gave me an earful about my chickens. I seriously thought about booking a room in cell block C for a couple of days until she cooled off. Come to think of it, that was pretty close to the end of our chicken-raising days.

Chicken Raising

Jinny Praying with the Fur Babies

Frank Riding Storm

22

Time to Get to Work

God waited long enough for me. It was time to get back to work. In the middle of spending all this time with the garden and the animals, I found some time to get over to the local courthouse. Once a week, I would go to the courthouse and spend time just praying. I sat in the very back of the courtroom, trying not to be obvious. The judge would have none of it. Every time I walked into the room, she eyeballed me up and down. After the second or third time, she asked me to come into her chambers. She wanted to know what business I had there. I told her I just came in there to pray on the children, that they would be represented fairly so that they would not end up in the system. I told her of my experience at Jackson prison working with young boys and how detrimental it was to the community and everybody else when one of these young boys ended up in the prison system. I asked her if it were possible that instead of sentencing these young boys for relatively minor offenses, if she could release them in my care on some kind of work-release program. I would work with them on community projects and teach them about my Jesus at the same time. She teared up and said that she and many people in her Bible study group had been praying for someone like me to come to their community and help these young men out. She started sending me boys to work with immediately.

At first, I would take them to local churches, parks, and businesses to do light cleanup work. We would take frequent breaks. During the breaks, I would ask them about what got them in the juvenile justice program. I would buy a few pizzas, and we would spend more time eating and talking than working. I told them stories about young men in the prison system who were in there because of bad choices they made. I got into detail, actually very graphic detail about what happened to these young boys in the prison system. They needed to know that when their friends stopped cheering them on and thinking that they were cool for spending months or years all alone either in prison or away from the comforts of home, these so-called friends of theirs would be nowhere in sight and they will have thrown away their future just to get the approval of some knucklehead.

In time, these young men would share with me nightmare stories of their childhood. They had been told that they were nothing and would amount to nothing, just like some previous relative. Many of them had an older brother, a cousin, or father in prison. Worse yet, some never met their fathers. Hope had been stolen from them before they even reached their teenage years. When I asked them what their future goals were, they answered with something like, "I just want to stay out of jail" or "I want to get me a truck and go hunting and fishing."

They needed to fill out a reporting form for the judge to receive credit for working off their probation hours. She could not make them come to my program. I made no false representations. This was about them developing a relationship with their God. I had found from my time working in the prison system that young men and women who did not have a personal relationship with the Lord would have close to a ninety percent recidivism rate. All they were doing with their time in jail was learning new tricks and tools on how to take advantage of the system they were caught up in. They were anxious to try out these new tricks and tools when they were released back into society. The ones who found this personal relationship or a real day-to-day relationship with Jesus, their recidivism rate dropped to less than forty percent. It was not perfect, but a heck of a lot better than any other program available in the justice system. The political nature in our government would not allow any funding that was faith-based because of some bureaucrat's interpretation of our constitution. The document does not say freedom from religion, it says freedom from a government-forced religion. One thing is for sure, when it comes to government-run institutions, change does not come easy and policy decisions never make sense. Just keep throwing billions of dollars at this failed policy that keeps churning out generations of career criminals when the perfect program was available for free, written by the highest court in the universe and authored by the Creator of it in the Holy Bible.

These kids had no one to answer to and felt that they were all alone in the world. They felt their decisions and choices had no effect on anybody at all. They could not see the choices they were making would determine the future of everyone around for the rest of their lives. When the results of their poor decisions made it to the local courts, it falls under the purview of the local sheriff. They would have a bull's-eye on their backs and become a future target when anything went wrong in their community. They needed to find a way to break the cycle of generational poverty and pain. The only way that I knew how to help them was to introduce them to my Jesus and make Him their Jesus as well. They need to live for something greater than themselves with hope for a future filled with all the good things their Father in heaven had in store for them. They had to know that all the things they saw other young men doing, prospering in, and growing up to be could be theirs as well. They needed to know that they were the sons and daughters of the King of kings and that made them joint heirs of all the kingdoms of God. They were not junk. They were prince and princesses on His kingdom. All they needed to do was claim their inheritance and live up to the standards that were set for them. They needed to find their true purpose in life, to serve their Creator and His Son, Jesus Christ. It was not about religion; it was always about a relationship with this guy named Jesus who would always be there for them and never leave them alone again. They could count on Him 24-7. He promised all of us that He would send the Comforter, His Holy Spirit. All the broken promises made to these young people from everybody they had known in the past no longer had to scar them for life. They would now have Jesus and this Holy Spirit wherever they went all the days of their life, if they could only find it in their heart to trust Him, ask Him for guidance, and give their hearts to Him.

The results of these conversations were incredible. Young men who had previously tried to come across as so "macho" would break down into tears. Tearing off the outer shells was not the most difficult thing to do, it was putting the pieces back together again and showing them from good examples of how real men serve this Lord and treat all the women in their lives. It was critical at this stage in their development that they looked at women as daughters of the King of kings, not just a challenge, a notch on their belt, or a conquest to be thrown aside when they were done with them. They needed to learn how to treat these women with respect, starting with girlfriends, sisters, mothers, and grandmothers. They also needed to learn that by giving respect, they would get the respect they so desperately needed in return.

I would sit and listen to these young men tell me their individual stories. In some cases, it may have been the first time any man had taken a personal interest in them. I let them know how important they were and that their opinion mattered. We would work on these opinions in the future. For now, they needed to know that they themselves had worth and somebody cared what they thought about things. We would discuss at length about choices. One of the first principles I taught them was that choices mattered and that they were where they were in life because of the choices they made or were made for them. If they wanted a different outcome in their lives, they would have to make wiser choices.

Word started spreading that this was not a bad way to spend their time so more and more young kids started to show up. The young men would come from all over the county, needing transportation, retired educators and other civic-minded people like Don and Joelle Kricheric, Rick Dafoe, Kirk Walton and a host of others rallied to provide transportation for these young boys and to help wherever they were needed. As the weather turned, we had nowhere to meet, so I had all the kids come to my house. Jinny had become a den mother, preparing meals, snacks, and drinks. We would spend time watching movies about changed lives. After each viewing, we would open up to have group discussions about what the young men had seen in these videos. My background in the restaurant business gave me the idea the young men needed to learn how to provide for themselves in the kitchen. One of my businesses was a pizzeria so I would teach the boys how to make pizzas from scratch. The trick was they would have to do it themselves. They loved this and would be so proud that they had made their favorite pizzas. We made other food as well. Spaghetti and meatballs, tacos, and nachos were other favorites. The young men, enjoying themselves, would ask if they could continue coming by even after they fulfilled their obligations to the court. The judge was working with me and would allow extra credit for the young men who would show up on their own.

I was at the court one day when the judge asked to speak to me. She said she wanted me to introduce me to a state trooper named Jamie Bullis. She asked him to develop a program for children based on the authentic manhood program that he was already teaching at a men's Bible study. She wanted him to change the format to fit young men. He accepted her challenge and began working on the program. When he was ready, she told him she wanted him to meet me and see if I could arrange for me to bring "my kids" to his program. Jamie and I were about as different as two men could be. Jamie was the real deal GI Joe type. Physically fit, he loved doing the craziest things like jumping out of perfectly good airplanes, diving with sharks in the ocean, and driving at speeds that defied common sense. Part of the canine unit, he was the trooper they called when things got too dicey for normal troopers. Drug busts or missing children? Call Jamie. Bear stuck in a tree in the middle of a busy town? Call officer Bullis. He would climb that tree and get that bear down. A straightforward kind of guy, he adhered to every law. The guy was nuts, but he loved the Lord, and he loved kids which worked for me.

He designed the program to last all summer long, twelve weeks in all. He had chosen a pavilion at a private club called Lost Lake Woods Club. It was a perfect location with outdoor archery ranges, trails, and a lake. The boys would be taught about Jesus, my main objective. Jamie would teach them survival skills, like how to purify water, identify what kind of plants and insects that were safe to eat, and build debris shelters. Basically, what to do if they were left all alone in the woods. At the end of the twelve-week program, if they passed all the attendance requirements, they would be taken on a seventy-two-hour adventure where they would be left alone in the woods and have to survive on their own. We almost lost them all when this plan revealed no cell phones, TVs, or computer games were allowed. All they could bring with them was the clothes on their back, a pocketknife, and a Bible. Jamie asked me if I would be spending the seventy-two hours with him and the kids out in the woods, I laughed at him. My idea of exercise was when I had to park my car more than a few spaces away from the front door of the grocery store. Hiking? Why would anyone want to do that if their car had not broken down? My idea of roughing it was the Red Roof Inn where they advertised sleep cheap. No, camping, not going to happen champ. He was cracking up.

On the very first night that I met Trooper Jamie Bullis, after he completed his class teaching these 20 or so young men, I approached him and told him that he needed to get rid of the Michigan State Trooper uniform he was wearing and go into full-time ministry. This boy could preach and, most importantly, he preached from the heart filled with the presence of the Holy Spirit. He was a life changer. He would even change mine. He would eventually become the son that God had never given me before, and I consider him to be one of the gifts God has given me. It is an honor to have this man in my life, his wife Joy, and his amazing family. There would come another young man very soon. I would then be blessed with two sons.

In the evenings, I would go out to the campsite bonfire where Jamie and the boys hung out, warmed up and hold a Bible study. The boys were learning to survive in a situation that they thought would be impossible just a few weeks prior. They were finding the confidence in themselves that they never knew existed. That got to enjoy sitting next to an inland lake that was reflecting the majesty of the star-filled sky on the water. They had no one to distract them for the first time in their lives, except the Creator of the universe. They learned lessons like how listening and following instructions could have life-changing consequences, even to the point of life and death.

Most importantly, they learned how important their relationship with the Lord was for all of eternity.

Earlier in the summer, a situation had arisen with one of the boys. In the grand scheme of things, it did not seem all that important, but it reminded me of a situation that I had encountered many years before when I was correcting a pastor of mine. He had a knack for telling his own version of the truth when giving his otherwise excellent sermons, that made the whole message unpalatable. I had heard this story from the pastor, which I now relayed to Jamie to incorporate it the final teaching of his seventy-two-hour weekend. The story was to enforce the importance of never letting even the smallest exception to occur in your speech or your value system. The story was called "Just a Little Bit of Poop."

It was about a Christian family whose children came home from school and asked their father for permission to meet some other kids at the mall that weekend. They wanted to see the latest movie that was just coming out at the theatre. The dad asked the kids, "What is the movie rated?" They replied that the movie was rated R just because of a few cuss words. There was also just one scene where this couple were getting undressed and climbing into bed when their parents came home, but nothing came of it. That is all and could you believe they rated the movie an R just for that? The father said, "Let me think about it for a day or two. I will let you know my decision."

The following day when the kids got off the bus from school, they noticed their father's car in the driveway. He never got home from work until several hours after they were home from school. They all rushed into the house to find their father in the kitchen with an apron around his waist. There were dirty pots and pans everywhere, but sitting on the kitchen table was a pile of triple chocolate brownies

*with several glasses of cold milk. They were starv-
ing and ran to the table to dig into those amazing
brownies when their dad stopped them.*

*"I have to tell you the story of my day first
before you can eat the brownies," he said. "I woke
up this morning after hardly being able to sleep last
night, thinking about you kids. I decided to take
the day off from work because I felt like I had been
neglecting my duties as your father. I decided I
wanted to do something especially nice for you. I
went to the market purchased the best ingredients I
could buy, the best Swiss chocolate, fresh eggs, sugar,
flower, cocoa powder, and an imported chocolate
icing. I came home and combined all the ingredients in the mixing bowel with all the love I could
incorporate into this mixture. Before I poured it into
the baking pan, I stopped for a moment, set the bowl
down, and took a teaspoon. Yes, just a teaspoon and
I went out into the backyard and picked up just a
teaspoon of your dog Sancho's poop. It was very fresh.
I brought it back in the kitchen and carefully added
it in the brownie mixture. I was sure to blend it in
very carefully. So now that you know how my day
went, go ahead and have your brownies and milk."*

*The kids began to get nauseous and objected
violently. "What is the matter with you? Why would
you ruin those beautiful brownies by putting poop
in them?" they asked. "No way are we going to eat
those. You have ruined them."*

*"That is just the same thing your mother and
I felt like when you told us that you wanted to go to
the movies and allow that crap into the perfection
that God created and that we love so much, our perfect children."*

Jamie's example was even more deliberate. After seventy-two hours in the woods with nothing to eat and only water to drink, he prepared a giant pot of venison stew that was cooking over the open fire when the boys came in to break camp. They probably were ready to eat the bark off the trees when Jamie made them sit through his telling of how he prepared this meal for them. Then he told them he found a pile of bear poop and put a scoop of it in the stew. We thought the boys would hurl what, if anything, was left in their stomachs. One boy couldn't care less. He said, "Give me a spoon." They understood the lesson.

That night, as the fire burned bright under a starlit sky, ten young men out of fourteen gave their hearts to the Lord and asked Jesus to let them live their lives for Him. Over the years, many more young men would follow in these boys' footsteps with The Chosen Ranch Ministries.

The First group of Boys who gave their hearts to the Lord

We were feeling rather good about ourselves with all the progress we were making with the children when, in one day, the wheels fell off. Jinny and I were home, and like hundreds of times before, we got into a little argument that escaladed. I could not even remember what this one was about, but we, opened the window and let the devil in. Previously, during another one of these emotional explosions of mine that I was having with Josh, a good friend of mine, Gina, was listening to me rant as she was on her phone to someone else, and when I opened the door to my office, I heard her describe it that "everybody better leave Frank alone because he was losing his Jesus." Well, this day, Jinny and me both were both losing our Jesus. Words were exchanged that no one who claims to be a Christian should ever have come out of their mouths. I was feeling that Jesus had left the house, when in the middle of the heat of this battle, the phone rang. I answered it with a grumpy voice, "Hello." I really did not want to be bothered.

On the other side of the phone, I heard in an exceptionally soft voice, even meekly, say, "Hello, Mr. Frank. You do not know me, but my name is Amber, and I am Jeff R.'s girlfriend. I am pregnant, and we are having relationship problems. Everybody we know have told us to call you and Miss Jinny for counselling to help save our relationship." Jinny was on the other side of the room, still fiery mad at me when I took the phone, held it to my chest, looked up as if to see God, and said, "You have got to be kidding me" at the top of my lungs. I brought the phone back to my ear and said, "Honey, it is not a good time for me," but she pleaded, saying they were out of time and they needed help now and they had no other place to go. She asked if they could come over now. I could not say no to her. "Come on over," I said.

I hung up and started to laugh. Jinny, still mad as all get out said, "What is going on?"

I told her that we would have to stop fighting because God had an assignment for us, and we would be doing marriage counseling in half an hour. We stared at each other in amazement as it sunk into us just how much our Lord loved us, and that He had just shown us again who we serve. We were laughing uncontrollably at how great this God is we serve. The kids arrived shortly, and we shared with them about the importance of having this third cord in any relationship, and his name was Jesus. After weeks of counselling with these kids, Jinny and I realized that the counseling was for us. Maybe not for this couple. They split up about a year later, and I was involved in getting his parents' custody of the baby boy, who are doing a wonderful job raising him. He calls me godfather.

23

The Call that Set Everything into Motion

It had been a long summer. I was ready for a good long rest. I had just taken a carload of boys to their homes. They were so energized by what they just experienced. They were not used to this type of friendship, care, and love shown to them. They were not ready to have it end. School was set to open for the fall semester, but the boys did not want to give up their newfound friends and asked when we were getting together again. At the time, we had no future plans so I said next summer. The boys objected and asked if we could have a weekly get-together, like a Bible study or something. How do you say no to a group of young men who want to study God's word together? I said, "Let me see what I can make happen." When I came home and told my wife what the boys asked, she said, "You have to do this for them." We put the word out that we would be holding weekly Bible studies Wednesday night at my house. Jamie worked most evenings so holding the Bible studies was going to be up to me. I started praying, asking for God's guidance. At the same time, Jamie was holding weekly men's Bible studies at his house, based on the authentic manhood lessons.

One afternoon, my phone rang. The call was coming from the courthouse by Tom Keller, a juvenile justice case worker. He said, "Frank, we have a problem." A grandfather who had custody of his grandson due to the fact that he put his own son, the boy's father, in prison for stealing from him had called the court. The grandfather, who had no desire to have anything to do with the young boy, told the judge that he was dropping him off at the court because he was leaving for Arizona. He brought the boy, along with a garbage bag of his clothes, and left him with Tom. At the time, there was not even one foster care home in the entire county. The boy would have to be sent to the other side of the state if they could not find a place to take this young man. His mother abandoned him when he was three or four years old. His father was just sent to prison for up to fifteen years. His grandfather, after telling him that he was useless and was going to end up just like his father in prison, dropped him off on the courthouse steps like he was piece of trash. My wife told me to get the young boy and bring him home. I did. Within another week, a second young boy called us, begging us to take him in as well.

This God we serve sure has a funny sense of timing. I had been praying for children for my entire life. Now at my old age, He decided that the timing was right to grant my wish. I knew both of these boys from the previous summer, working with them in the court-suggested program where they both were given community service hours for minor behavioral issues. Kenny, the first boy, was a no-brainer. He had no other place to go. The second boy, Ben...well, his situation broke my heart as well. When that call came, Ben was crying and asked if I could come and get him. He wanted to live with us because the fighting was getting so bad in his home that he was afraid of what would happen next. I told him I had to check with the court and would get back to him. He said, "Please hurry!"

I went to the courthouse and talked to, in my opinion, the two women who kept that place running. If anybody could get something done, it was either of them. Pam Ashford and Gail Leeseberg are two of God's angels who work in underappreciated capacities but are the heart and soul of our entire county. They are God-loving women who had a real heart for the children and families they worked with in the family court system. When I told them that Ben called, they were elated that he would be getting out of his horrible living situation. They gave me the paperwork and told me to hurry and go get him. They said I would have to get both of his parents to sign off, basically give up their parental rights to me. This task would be next to impossible because Ben had not even seen his dad in quite a while and his mother was fighting her addiction to marijuana. However, all of us knew that God would make a way. His mother always had a houseful of druggies over and was moving from new boyfriend to new boyfriend. His parents split up in a very nasty divorce. Ben's older brother was in jail in Las Vegas. He and his sister hated each other. Pam and Gail said that if I could get back before five in the afternoon, they would get the judge to sign the order, giving Jinny and I temporary full custody. He lived on the other side of the county. I called Jinny and told her I would be picking her up. I also called my new friend Kirk, a retired EMT, and asked him to come with us. I needed backup, just in case Ben was hurt. I knew that Kirk could help with that. He was big and strong enough to keep me from going crazy on anybody who dared hurt that boy. Knowing Kirk better now, that was not the wisest choice. He loved these kids so much, he probably would have ended up in jail right alongside me if things had gone wrong.

When we arrived at his house, Ben was waiting anxiously for us. His mother was there with a few friends. The house reeked with the smell of marijuana and cat urine. When Ben told her that he wanted to come and live with us, she was crying but knew it was the best thing for him. She signed the papers instantly without even reading them. Jinny accompanied Ben into his bedroom to pack. He began scooping up clothes that were piled up in the corner that had been urinated on by several cats. He grabbed things like souvenirs, several guns, knives, and a pair of boots into garbage bags and loaded them into my truck. He said good-bye and climbed into the back seat of the truck with Jinny.

It would be the saddest thing that I had ever experienced looking in my rearview mirror as this boy looked back at his mother and the home that he had known, who had just signed him away like he was a used car so that she could enjoy her marijuana. It was difficult for me to drive as my eyes were filled with tears. We turned the corner and drove through the little town. I told Ben that we would have to find his father and get him to sign the documents too, which was going to be nearly impossible. He said he had not seen his father in years. About two miles down the road, Ben shouted, "Oh my god, that was my dad who just drove by!" I turned around and followed his truck to where he pulled into a house he was staying at. Ben's sister was also in that truck.

I told Ben to stay put. I got out of my truck and approached the man. He was alarmed as I approached and took a defensive posture. I introduced myself and told him that I had his son in my truck and what my objectives were. I produced the papers that I needed him to sign. His daughter objected. She said to him, "You do not even know this guy, do not sign anything.| I told him this was a one-time opportunity for Ben to have something of a normal life. He reasoned with his daughter, saying it had to be better than to leave Ben in that house with his mother. I turned around to get Ben and told him to say hello to his father. You could see the outward disdain that he had for his father, but he did ask him to sign the papers so that he could have a chance in life. The man signed the papers on the spot. In less than an hour and a half, I had custody of this young man. I called the courthouse they told me they would wait for me, even though it was after 5:00 PM and would get the order signed first thing in the morning. How great is this God we serve, a miracle maker!

I do not know how many of you have ever tried to adopt a pet dog or cat from the humane society. At times, their background checks could take days to make sure that you will be a good adaptive parent for the pets. The irony that I could have attained guardianship of this young man in one and a half hours is just beyond my comprehension to this day.

24

Confirmation from God

There was a bigger plan in the works. I just did not know what it was yet. I had been going to Jamie's house once a week for his men's bible study and if ever I needed guidance it was now. I had just committed to raising two teenage boys. My neighbor Rick and I headed over to Jamie's to attend the study and he could tell I was not myself. We arrived after the forty-five-minute ride in silence and entered the house. We were the last ones to arrive so Jamie would usually start the study by praying and asking if anyone needed specific prayer that we could all come to the Lord for. When it came to me, I asked the guys to pray and pray hard. I needed a sign from God that very night on what direction He wanted me to take with these boys. I asked that if it be His will for us to continue with this mission to show me how we were to proceed and if it was not His will to put the biggest bolder in front of me before I destroyed a lot of lives. We all prayed. Jamie keyed up the DVD player and we began our lesson on the Authentic Manhood series. At the very end of this week's segment the DVD played on and segued into an infomercial. It was about a guy by the name of John Croyle from Alabama who opened up a Ranch for abandoned abused and neglected children 40 years ago and to date he and his organization called The Big Oak Ranch had raised over 2000 children in a Christ Centered Environment of homes staffed by what he called house parents. Tears ran down the faces of all 8 guys who were at the bible study and we all knew that we had just heard from the Almighty Himself. Jamie got on the phone and planned for a group of us to head to Alabama and see what they had going on. We were to leave in three weeks.

We were all on a mission now. Jamie took us to look at a friend of his hunting lodge to see if it would be an appropriate home to raise children. While it was beautiful and the land was more than adequate it just did not feel right. Another friend of mine that had been looking at a rather large piece of property about a year ago had told me that they had lost interest dealing with the divorcee who owned the parcel and had given up pursuing it. I asked if they would mind if I made an inquire about this property. They said go ahead but warned me again about trying to work with this woman. I took our whole team out to take a look around the property and we prayed all over the place. We agreed that we would make an offer even though the place was way out of our budget. There were 160 acres of land with two ponds and the Black River ran right through it. A big beautiful house with a two-story carriage barn and a horse barn with fenced pasture. The perfect place to raise boys. I called the realtor. She came right out to show us the inside of the house and outbuildings. I had pre-arranged with the team that if they all agreed that this was the place to give me the thumbs up sign and I would take the realtor to a local restaurant and write the purchase agreement. Everyone fell in love with the place and all thumbs were up. The realtor drove separately to the restaurant, we acquired a back booth out of the way, and she took out her forms to begin to fill them out. She felt compelled to tell me that she would be so glad to be done with this piece of property for the same reasons my friends told me about the homeowner. She drives me crazy the realtor exclaimed. The woman will just not listen to reason. I knew this because I had done my homework and found out that the property had gone into a sheriff's sale for non-payment of taxes and bank payments. I had been praying for a number to offer from the Lord and I settled on one and resolved not to go up a single dollar. If this were what He wanted for us He could make it work. After she had filled in all the details of our name, address, phone etc. etc. she asked what the amount was that we were offering. The number I told her almost launched her out of her seat. She was so angry with me and said that I was wasting her time. You heard what I said about this woman she will never accept that amount. In fact, she turned down a cash offer of much more than this just the month before she added. I said to her my friend, I have been in Real Estate and I know the rules. You are obligated to present all offers and this is the number that the guy I work for (Jesus) gave me to present. He does not take no for an answer too many times, if it is what He wants. I will wait for her response. She tossed the paperwork into her briefcase and said the women lives out of state and it could take about a week for her to get back with me. I said take your time. the following day my phone rang and it was the realtor. You are not going to believe it. I said yes, I will, my boss, Jesus, already told me this morning while I was praying that it was a done deal. She said oh my God your right. She accepted your offer. The miracles were just starting and the work of His Almighty hand would continue to reveal themselves. The property was once purchased for twice what we just got it for.

The following day I went to the bank that held the note that was in foreclosure figuring it would be the easiest place to get approved for that large a mortgage since they would see me as fresh meat that they could attach to their already bad loan. I spoke to a Vice-President so I could cut out the middlemen and he gave me a loan application and started running a credit check on me. I came home and filled out the forms and made an extra copy for myself. On the way back down to the bank I stopped at my own financial institution, Northland Area Federal Credit Union in Oscoda Michigan. While in line to see a teller, I struck up a conversation with a young lady who was in management. I told her I needed to move some of my funds around and would like a cashier's check for the deposit on this property we were buying. She looked at me and asked why don't you apply for the loan with us. I told her my theory about the other bank already holding the bad note and she said, that does not matter, give us an opportunity. I said ok and I gave her my extra copy of the loan application. I left and proceeded to the next town and went in and saw the Vice-President again. He took my application and said he was leaving for vacation at the end of the week so he would try and walk the application through their underwriting department before he left. I said great and left the bank and headed home. I hated to waste the nice ladies time at Northland so I stopped in and told her that the other bank would have me approved in just a few days. She looked me in the eye as if to see if I were pulling her leg and when she figured I was sincere she hesitated for a second and told me she would have me approved by that afternoon. Her name is Wendy and she has been my go-to gal ever since. And she loves the Lord. True to her word she called me that afternoon with the approval. I had never seen anything like this in all of my time selling real estate.

Now I needed to get an inspection done on the property, all the outbuildings and all 5 wells on the place before the end of the week. Wendy had given me the names of three inspection companies and one sounded familiar. I called them and talked to a young man whom I had met on a different occasion and I told him who I was and what we were planning to do with this property including finding a set of Christian house parents to raise the children. He told me if I could wait until Friday, he would come out himself and save us a ton of money. I said that would be fine. When I told him where the property was, he said that is funny, I am the caretaker of a piece of property over there. It would turn out that this was the place he had been cutting the grass and taking care of for years. What a coincidence, or was it? On Friday I walked the property with him in the bitter cold and when we got inside he remarked that he had brought his wife out here before and they dreamed about doing the same thing we were going to do with this place. Take in kids and raise them alongside there own3 children. I invited him and his wife out the following day for a bonfire and a prayer service that our little team was going to have at the property. He said they would come and then he asked me to please not to mention to his wife about the houseparent thing. I said no problem. The following day we were all huddled out in the cold around the makeshift fire pit we constructed and we began praying and I was filled with the Holy Spirit. I walked over to the young inspector's wife, her name is Sara and I laid a hand on her shoulder and asked her to go home and pray about being our new house parents. Her husband Josh, with a stunned look on his face just looked at me and laughed. They had heard from the Lord the night before and already had accepted the assignment. That night God gave me my second son. Jamie, Josh, and I would become closer than birth relatives. God had a definite purpose for our lives.

25

On Our Way to Big Oak Ranch in Alabama

It was time, Jamie's shift was over, he would be off for the next couple of days. We had the van packed and were on our way to Alabama to visit John Croyle and the Big Oak Ranch. John was a former All-American defensive end for the University of Alabama who gave up a promising carrier playing football in the NFL to follow his calling of creating a Christian home for abandoned, abused, and neglected young children over forty years ago. We drove straight through to the Big Oak Ranch from upstate Michigan. I thought it would be an easy ride with having four drivers, but one young fella never drove and the professional state trooper slept most of the way, and complained about my driving when he was awake. His new favorite pastime was making fun of me. That was fine. I was rather good at dishing it out so I had to be able to take the ribbing from the young puppy too. When he was not snoring, he was pretty amusing. We laughed a lot, making the travel much easier, except when I missed a turn (it was my navigator's fault, of course). I drove over sixty miles in the wrong direction before we figured it out and had to backtrack, adding 120 miles to what was a long trip to start with. I never heard the end of it. We checked into the nice cabin our hosts arranged for us, showered, and changed clothes before our first meeting with Mr. Croyle. The place was incredible two-story brick homes, with well-manicured lawns, in a beautiful setting. A large horse arena with pastures, and wonderful common areas surrounding an inland lake. I was blown away. This was much more than I anticipated.

John addressed this right off the bat. His kids deserve some of the finer things in life after everything they had been through. He would have nothing but the best for his kids. He personally escorted us through the whole complex and then took us several miles to their academy. He told us the story of how he started out with just five of the roughest toughest kids he ever meet. The locals kind of looked down on him and his boys. When the local officials came to inquire what was he doing and if he had a license to operate, he answered, "Yes, sir." When they demanded to see his license, he took out his wallet, showed them his driver's license. That was the only license he had. "When had it become against the law to love your fellowman." I loved the guy. He and I instantly bonded.

We arrived at the Westbrook Christian School that was once a closed-down elementary school they acquired for $1. They transformed it into a K-12 grade school that surpassed any public school I have ever been into. It was near lunchtime. The kids all poured into the cafeteria and came rushing up to Mr. John to give him a hug or tell him their exciting news of the day. He introduced us to the children, tell them who you are. They put out their little hands and said, "Hello, my name is… It is a pleasure to meet you" and shook our hands. Then they gave John another big hug and hurried off for lunch. The meals the kids were eating looked wonderful but they had a special table set up for us in the same room where we could observe the children at dinner that their chefs prepared for us. It was amazing.

John was so welcoming and fun to be with. He was no stranger to trash-talking too. He asked us if we were ever going to get a real football team in Michigan and if the Detroit Lions still had to purchase their own tickets to the Super Bowl. It was common knowledge that our beloved Lions were bad, but I still loved them and defended them. He asked us plenty of questions about our organization, how many volunteers we had, and where we were located. You could tell he had been through many meetings like this in over forty years of loving on kids. He said that if we got started as soon as we got back home, we were at least two years away from acquiring any children after we had found and acquired the land and buildings we would need to get started. He sensed something was amiss by the looks we gave each other. I told him that we just purchased the 160-acre property that we were going to call it The Chosen Ranch right out of Ephesians 1 in the Bible. That we already had two teenage boys living with me at home, ready to move into the ranch when the upgrades were complete. He was amazed. He said we were light years ahead of where he was at in the startup process. He was excited for us but issued some warnings. Looking right into my eyes, he said, "Stay focused. Don't let the enemy—who comes to lie, kill, and destroy—distract you from your God-given purpose. You're going to need to know what you are willing to give up to do this job well. You can't be pulled in too many directions to be truly effective. There are people who will not want you to succeed, cut them loose. Others will come alongside you for only a short time or a season. Some will be there for a lifetime, treasure them all. Do not get discouraged." He then handed me a copy of his book, *Who You Are*, and signed it with these words, "Frank, thank you for wanting to make a difference. Signed, John Croyle." He then added the passage from Romans 8:28, "And we know that in all things God works for the good of those who love Him, who have been called according to His purpose." As we parted ways, he added, "Just be yourself, read your Bible, pray, and trust the Holy Spirit."

Throughout my life, I never elevated many people to hero status. I think it is a term that has been watered down from overuse, sometimes given so trivially to people who could bounce a ball, throw a touchdown, or hit a curve ball. My heroes were my dad Alphonse Dimercurio, my mentor and friend Louie Morabito, and now Hall of Famer John Croyle. You will never know in this world, how big a difference that twenty-four hours I spent with you made in the direction of my life. I eternally thank you.

26

Serving Christ

I am big on having a plan and following that plan. This probably comes from all the time in my life that I was clueless and did not have a plan. Serving Christ is the most important goal any person could ever have. There is no greater reward in all heaven or earth than to know that the creator of the universe chose you to achieve one of his purposes. They have not invented a trophy or a reward of any size or shape that can surpass this honor.

We spend much time with the children at the ranch, talking about the future and what it holds for them. Their past, no matter how horrible or frustrating, means nothing anymore. From the day they come to us, it is all about the bright future they will have for all eternity, living for and with Jesus Christ. Each and every one of us, and there are so many that I could not list all the great people who have come together to make the Chosen Ranch what it is today, have a story to tell about that special life-changing moment or child that they hold near and dear to them.

We are always telling the kids, "Make a plan and work the plan. You can always change the plan, but if you do not have one, you will never have a direction to take." Also, above all else, never leave the Lord out of your plans. He will never leave you or forsake you. Do not leave him.

I do not like to single out any one young man because they are all so special to me and are all my gifts from God. But I am going to do it here. This young boy, Damian, came to us early on when we were meeting in my living room. His entire family had been through some unspeakable difficulties, and he and his brothers and sisters were transported to my house by a wonderful elderly couple named Don and Joelle Krecheric, who knew this family's whole story. Through the years, they all just stayed with our programs and became a part of the family.

One day, I received a call from one of our volunteers; he told me that there was another boy that we needed to bring to live at the ranch. When I inquired further who was this boy, I was told it is Damian. I had not seen Damian all summer long and I was confused. "What is going on?"

Damian had left his home because, well it depended on who you talked to for the real reason, but he was living all over the place and had not eaten in weeks. I went and found him, and he looked like he was ready to pass out. I called a friend of mine who was the administrator at the local health center, and she worked her magic at 6:00 pm on a Friday night and found a doctor that I could get him in to see. My wife, Jinny, called Sara Whitten, our house mom, and we all met up at the doctor's office. Once inside, the doctor began to examine Damian and found that his blood sugar level was dangerously low. He passed out right there when they went to take his blood. The doctor had left the room and had been gone for a while when I decided to go looking for him. He was on the phone with child protective services, telling them that he thought we were the cause of Damion's abuse. I told the doctor he had the story wrong; we had just picked him up. The doctor gave him some juice and some medicine, and he started doing better. I asked Damian why he had not come to me before. He knew how many kids we had helped, and he answered that he just thought he was not worth the trouble. He said there were so many more worthy kids out there than him.

I held him in my arms and told him there was not one kid in the world that was more worthy than him, and we took him home, and the Whitten's have raised him ever since. Damian has been one of the best ambassadors of our program we have ever had. He was out cutting grass on a zero-turn lawnmower in the village when he came across an older widow woman who was struggling with her groceries in the trunk of her car. Damian stopped what he was doing and approached the woman; she was scared at first, but then she let him carry all her groceries in the house for her. When she went to tip him, he told her, "No, thank you, ma'am. That is not what we are about at the Chosen Ranch."

I had always said, "If God had us do everything that we had done in our years for the Ranch, and even if it were for just one young soul, it would have all been worthwhile." This was the soul. The next week or two later, Damian came into my office and asked to speak to me. I said, "Sure, come on in."

He said, "You know how you are always on us about having a plan for our lives."

I said, "Yes."

He said, "I have found the job I want to have when I grow up."

I said, "Okay, what is it?"

He said, "I want your job. I want to run the Chosen Ranch."

I held him and cried. "I have never had a better compliment in my life."

27

The Day of the Lord

And afterward, I will pour out my Spirit on all peo-
ple. Your sons and daughters will prophesy, your old
men will dream dreams, your young men will see
visions.

—Joel 2:28 (NIV)

Before we even purchased the ranch property, I received a call from Tom McCuish, a fraternity brother from my first year at the University of Detroit who accompanied me that day we went to the orphanage and had our Easter celebration for the kids. At that time, Tom's father owned and operated several Christian homes providing end-of-life care for elderly people. He wished me a Merry Christmas while I was visiting my mother and sisters for the holidays. I always admired Tom for all he did for that population of people and I shared the dream that kept coming to me night after night of starting a Ranch for kids. He hung up the phone and drove across town, handed me a check, and told me get started. A few weeks later, I used that check as the deposit for the purchase of The Chosen Ranch. That check was a gift from God. It had made its way full circle.

Our offer had been accepted. I was now standing on the back porch of the ranch house and looking out at the vast acres of land overrun with Russian olive bushes and scrub trees. With the wind howling and snow blowing into my face, I looked out, but I saw none of this. A warmth enveloped my body as I saw a vision of beautiful well-manicured grass, fruit trees loaded with fruit, and flowers everywhere. I viewed horses running over the hillside and a garden of vegetables. White-tailed deer perked up to see what was going on. Rabbits and turkeys were roaming all over the woods. The sound of children's laughter filled the air as a band played praise and worship music in the background. I could smell barbeque cooking on open grills as car after car of friends and well-wishers lined down the half-mile driveway to join a backyard filled to near capacity of people sitting in lawn chairs for as far as I could see. Young boys driving tractors, pulling flatbed trailers with square bales of hay being towed around the property with folks sitting on them, giving the people tours of their home. I looked in the sky and saw a bald eagle circling above. For a moment, I saw the face of my Lord and Savior Jesus Christ smiling from above.

Nine months later, after thousands of volunteer hours from people all over our community, Josh and Sara Whitten moved into the ranch with their three children and the first two of several children that would follow. Shortly after, late one night I would get a phone call from Sara. She said, "Frank, I know we are a boy's ranch for now until we can afford to buy another property to build a ranch for girls, but we have a problem. A young girl, sixteen years old, is here right now and asked if she could just come in and maybe take a shower. She was living in her car and did not want to go to school dirty the next day. She had heard about us." I told Sara to bring her in, feed her, and give her a place to sleep. If the Lord led her to us, He expected us to take care of his child. This story repeated itself several times since. We added a community center right in town where kids from the area can come after school to hang out, get something to eat, join a Bible study, or attend our weekly youth group meetings. We take the kids sledding, skiing, and ice fishing in the winter, Christmas caroling during the holidays, and doing community service projects. We started a property management division where we cut grass, do spring and fall cleanups, and assist the local churches and seniors with household projects. We are on our way to becoming the second-best home for children in America because I promised John Croyle that we would never outdo him.

I have had my share of health issues over the years, including several heart attacks, two open-heart surgeries, and stomach bleeds from physicians practicing their craft and the science of their day and I have been clinically dead three times. My friends joke that it is all God saying that things are just too perfect in heaven to risk letting me in just yet on the oft change that all hell will break loose when I get there. I also know that it is all God. He is not done with me yet. I will not be going anywhere until He is done using me for His purpose. The following fall, my vision would become a reality. An old Greek proverb says, "A society grows great when old men plant trees whose shade they know they shall never sit in." This was the prayer I lifted up to my Lord and Savior Jesus Christ that He would just give me the time to plant the seeds of The Chosen Ranch. He was not only granting my wish, he was this day, giving me the opportunity to sit in the shade of His tree. Over five hundred people showed up to celebrate the anniversary of our opening The Chosen Ranch. Pastors brought their congregations out to mix with state dignitaries. We had letters written by judges, congressmen, and pastors from around the state sealed up and placed in a cornerstone time capsule in the wall of the house. We dedicated the property to our Lord. Speeches were made. Then it happened. The vision I had that cold and snowy day became a reality. The sounds of voices lifting up praise to God, the smells of barbeque, the laughter of children, our boys driving the tractor and touring people all around the property, and horses and Jerusalem donkeys whinnying in the pasture. I looked up with tears of joy streaming down my face to see not one, but two bald eagles circling overhead. How great is our God!

Christmas at the Chosen Ranch

28

Epilogue

This has been my story. I hope you found it worthwhile to read. More importantly, I hope you could find some nuggets of truth to apply to the challenges in your own life. Life is not easy, and the Christian life even more so. It was never promised to be easy. We all have challenges; some are harder than others. I am so grateful to my Lord and Savior Jesus Christ that He took that cross for me. Father God has forgiven me all my trespasses yesterday, today, and tomorrow. He still has not given up hope in mankind. He can still find a use for someone who has turned away from Him so many times. He has blessed me far greater than I ever deserved. I am grateful that He sent the Comforter, His Holy Spirit, to take up residence in my heart, to guide me from making too many mistakes again, and to have led so many wonderful children of His to His Chosen Ranch.

Now I want to leave you with a gift. I wish I could say it was from me, but it is not. I only wish that I could have received this gift early on in my life. Trying to live without this gift for a great portion of my life has been a nightmare, as you have just read. This gift is from your Father in heaven, brought to you by His Son, Jesus Christ. This gift is the gift of salvation for all eternity. The price of this gift is...well, priceless. You will never get a gift like it in your entire life. All you have to do to claim this gift is to receive Jesus as your Lord and Savior. To do this is simple, just repeat after me:

> *Dear God, I know that my sin has separated me from You. Thank You that Jesus Christ died in my*

place. I ask Jesus to forgive my sin and to come into my life. Please begin to direct my life. Thank You for giving me eternal life. In Jesus's name, amen

If you just prayed that prayer for the first time, welcome into the family of believers. Now the fun begins. Boy, does He have a plan for you! I hope your journey will be as fulfilling and rewarding as mine has been. Get ready because He will know if you really mean it. You are in for the ride of your life. Now I want to leave you with the question He asked me.

ARE YOU GOING TO MOVE WHEN HE TELLS *YOU* TO MOVE?

Frank and Jinny

www.ChosenRanch.org
P.O. Box 190 Lincoln, Michigan 48742
(989)335-Hope

About the Author

Frank Dimercurio has not gained any national recognition as a preacher or teacher of Christian values or principles. He is just a man who cried out to God to use him in a way that would be pleasing to Him. Like so many other people, Frank desired to live a life of purpose even though his path led him down many bad roads. With Jesus's example of using twelve very ordinary—or some would say, substandard—men to change the world, Frank figured that with the help of the Holy Spirit, he could assemble a small group of people and make a difference for the cause of Christ.

Frank is the executive director of The Chosen Ranch, a Christian home and ministry for children who need a second chance, located in Harrisville, Michigan. For more information, visit our website at www. ChosenRanch.org.

CPSIA information can be obtained
at www.ICGtesting.com
Printed in the USA
LVHW090250210221
679519LV00011B/300/J

9 781098 081843